Praise for *The Baptismal River*

Rev. Davenport's study is a pleasant surprise. He develops the richness of Baptism from the Old Testament, integrating theological themes with the New Testament. He makes excellent use of Scripture, the Confessions, and theologians to answer relevant questions about Baptism. He provides congregationally appropriate rules for interpretation, exegesis, apologetics, typology, and polemics. While describing the fullness of Baptism, he integrates Christology, pneumatology, original sin, justification, sanctification, faith, the Lord's Supper, and the Church. Davenport also relates Baptism's gifts to liturgy, hymnody, church history, pastoral care, and home life. Including its helpful illustrations and analogies, *The Baptismal River* is a little gem.

—Rev. Tim Beck, St. Paul Lutheran Church, Milford, Ohio

"There is a river whose streams make glad the city of God" (Psalm 46:4). Seeing that river and returning to its renewing waters is the aim of Rev. Richard Davenport's Bible study, *The Baptismal River*. Using especially Old Testament events that foreshadow the baptismal flood in Christ, the study provides the participant with all the gifts that God promises through Baptism, which "assuredly means forgiveness, but it also means quite a bit more." Through *The Baptismal River*, the reader will be submerged in all the wonders of our life-giving Trinity that the baptismal flood delivers.

—Rev. Dr. Kent J. Burreson, professor of systematic theology, Concordia Seminary, St. Louis

THE BAPTISMAL RIVER

STUDYING THE SACRAMENT THROUGHOUT SCRIPTURE

RICHARD DAVENPORT

CONCORDIA PUBLISHING HOUSE · SAINT LOUIS

Published by Concordia Publishing House
3558 S. Jefferson Avenue, St. Louis, MO 63118-3968
1-800-325-3040 • cph.org

Manufactured in the United States of America

Library of Congress Cataloging-in-Publication Data

Names: Davenport, Richard A., author.
Title: The Baptismal river : studying the sacramental throughout scripture / Richard A. Davenport.
Description: Saint Louis, MO : Concordia Publishing House, [2023] | Summary: "Baptismal theology has been woven throughout the pages of the Bible and human history from the beginning. The author will delve into biblical events and themes such as the flood, creation, the image of God, anointing, circumcision, and Jesus' Baptism to examine Baptism from an Old Testament perspective. As he examines these events, he will draw parallels to avoid reading into the biblical events things we already believe about Baptism. Participants will learn what God is doing in these stories and understand their baptismal connection"-- Provided publisher.

Identifiers: LCCN 2022060993 (print) | LCCN 2022060994 (ebook) | ISBN 9780758671134 (paperback) | ISBN 9780758671141 (ebook)
Subjects: LCSH: Baptism--Lutheran Church.
Classification: LCC BX8073.5 .D38 2023 (print) | LCC BX8073.5 (ebook) | DDC 234/.161--dc23/eng/20230411
LC record available at https://lccn.loc.gov/2022060993
LC ebook record available at https://lccn . l o c . g o v / 2 0 2 2 0 6 0 9 9 4

---

2 3 4 5 6 7 8 9 10 32 31 30 29 28 27 26 25 24

Table of Contents

STUDENT GUIDE

LEADER GUIDE

Student Guide

UNIT 1

Introduction

What is Baptism? This may sound like a rather ridiculous question for anyone who has been confirmed in the Lutheran Church. "It's a Means of Grace," you might say. Or perhaps it's "water and the Word." Both are true. If you really remember your Small Catechism, you might even pull out Luther's great statement: "It works forgiveness of sins, rescues from death and the devil, and gives eternal salvation to all who believe this, as the words and promises of God declare" (Baptism, Second Part).

It can't really be much simpler than that, can it? Luther sums it up pretty nicely there. It sounds pretty great. I mean, who wouldn't want all that stuff, especially when all you have to do is get a little wet? Maybe, though, if you spend any time really thinking about it, you might find yourself wondering, "How does Baptism do all this stuff?" You could go back to your Small Catechism again and find that answer that says it's God's Word along with the water that does such great things, but that's not really the question. Obviously, God can do whatever He wants any way He wants to do it. So why Baptism? What makes it so special? Why did He decide to do things this way? We have to be a little careful because God doesn't always reveal the hows and whys of what He does. But if it really is that important, you'd think He'd explain it a bit.

I'll throw you another curveball to really get things rolling. Are you sure Baptism actually is special? I mean *really* sure? Do you really need

Baptism at all?

Let's keep all this in the back of our minds for a moment and take a look at a couple of Bible passages and discuss them.

- Read 1 John 1:5–10.

1. **What does John say God does for those who confess their sins to Him?**

- Read Psalm 32:1–5.

2. **What does King David say was the result of his confession?**

If you're familiar with the historic Lutheran liturgy, you might recognize these passages and their connection to Confession and Absolution. Both passages affirm God's free grace. They both acknowledge how willing God is to forgive. John tells us forgiveness is God's natural response to our confession of sins. In his commentary on 1 John, Dr. Bruce Schuchard says,

> Here, then, in simple terms and without argument John states that, because Jesus is in all things faithful, because he himself is the embodiment of righteousness, we can in all things rely on him. At times, some have surmised that God would have to forget the righteous demands of the Law in order to forgive, like some feeble old man who, both consciously and unconsciously, overlooks many of the faults of those he loves.

> And yet nothing could be further from the truth. Jesus forgives precisely because he can be counted upon in every way to keep his word and at the same time to accomplish and to be what is right. Indifference toward sin is no act of faithfulness; forgiving sin is, on account of the Son's own willing sacrifice of his blood for those he loves.[1]

King David also remarks that God heard his confession, God forgave that sin, and David counts it a great blessing. Luther says of Psalm 32:5,

> This is in contrast to those in whom deceit of the spirit produces such false confidence that they can unabashedly justify and excuse themselves. Because of this they get into quarrels with other people and lapse into pride, anger, hatred, impatience, condemning, and slander. Their innocence makes them really guilty, and yet they claim to have done justly and rightly and to have acted fairly. They conceal deeply their own iniquity, for they look at their own righteousness and do not confess their sins to God sincerely and without deceit of the inner spirit. Righteous people, however, do not hide their iniquity, do not become angry, do not grow impatient even when they are wronged; for they do not feel that they can be wronged, since they find no righteousness in themselves. These are the blessed to whom God remits iniquity and cancels it because they confess it. Since they do not hide and cover their sin, God covers and hides it.[2]

- Read Matthew 18:21–35.

1 Bruce G. Schuchard, *1–3 John*, Concordia Commentary (St. Louis: Concordia Publishing House, 2012), 141.
2 Martin Luther, *Luther's Works*, vol. 14 (St. Louis: Concordia Publishing House, 1958), 150.

3. **What does the parable say about God's willingness to forgive and the magnitude of what He is willing to forgive?**

Peter asks Jesus an honest question about how forgiveness works, and Jesus responds with one of His helpful parables. If the master forgives a servant, and that servant is not willing to forgive another, it suggests the first servant never really thought much of that forgiveness to begin with.

In his commentary on Matthew, Dr. Jeffrey A Gibbs explains,

> Although Jesus' response makes it clear that Peter's understanding of the scope of forgiveness is inadequate, we should not fail to notice that by normal human standards, his offer to forgive a brother who sins against him up to seven times is not a trivial one. Nevertheless, whatever normal standard is guiding Peter's question is dwarfed and then swallowed up by the Christ's response.[3]

The debt owed by the first servant is such that he would have to work for a thousand years or more to pay it off. It is truly a debt that goes beyond all comprehension and yet the master, who we are meant to equate with Jesus Himself, simply forgives the debt and wipes it off the ledger. God's grace astounds us in both its quantity and quality. He forgives all sins, and He forgives all sins every single time a sinner confesses them, without exception.

In the Small Catechism, Luther says, "What is Confession?" Answer: "Confession has two parts. First, that we confess our sins, and second, that we receive absolution, that is, forgiveness, from the pastor as from God

3 Jeffrey A. Gibbs, *Matthew 11:2–20:34*, Concordia Commentary (St. Louis: Concordia Publishing House, 2010), 933–34.

Himself, not doubting, but firmly believing that by it our sins are forgiven before God in heaven" (Confession, "What is Confession?"). God forgives and is always ready to forgive. God is willing to forgive all sins, no matter what those sins are. He proves it by sending His Son to pay the debt, ensuring no sin would ever be too great to be beyond forgiveness.

That leads to a rather serious problem when we start talking about Baptism. If I can confess my sins to God and know He forgives them, just as we do in a worship service, then why do I need Baptism? Having another source of forgiveness might make sense if Absolution only covered certain sins, but God's forgiveness covers all sins, all the time. If God thought Baptism was so important that He commands us to continue doing it when we already have His forgiveness through Absolution, then perhaps it's because Baptism is doing things a bit differently. Over the next few sessions, we'll take a look at some of the events in the Bible that help us understand what Baptism is. By looking at what God has done in the past to prepare the world for Baptism, we'll see that God has some very special things going on in Baptism. When we fit all these pieces together, you'll get a glimpse of why the Church has called Baptism one of the sacred mysteries and how much God is doing for you through this gift.

Further in Depth

Luther says,

> You ask, "How does baptism help me, if it does not altogether blot out and remove sin?" This is the place for a right understanding of the sacrament of baptism. This blessed sacrament of baptism helps you because in it God allies himself with you and becomes one with you in a gracious covenant of comfort.
>
> In the first place you give yourself up to the sacrament of baptism and to what it signifies. That is, you desire to die, together

> with your sins, and to be made new at the Last Day. This is what the sacrament declares, as has been said. God accepts this desire at your hands and grants you baptism. From that hour he begins to make you a new person. He pours into you his grace and Holy Spirit, who begins to slay nature and sin, and to prepare you for death and the resurrection at the Last Day.
>
> In the second place you pledge yourself to continue in this desire, and to slay your sin more and more as long as you live, even until your dying day. This too God accepts. He trains and tests you all your life long, with many good works and with all kinds of sufferings. Thereby he accomplishes what you in baptism have desired, namely, that you may become free from sin, die, and rise again at the Last Day, and so fulfill your baptism. Therefore we read and see how bitterly he has let his saints be tortured, and how much he has let them suffer, in order that, almost slain, they might fulfill the sacrament of baptism, die, and be made new. For when this does not happen, when we do not suffer and are not tested, then the evil nature gains the upper hand so that a person invalidates his baptism, falls into sin, and remains the same old man he was before.[4]

Baptism is certainly a singular moment in a Christian's life. Coming to the font and receiving that gift of grace is a life-changing event. But that doesn't mean everything God does in Baptism begins and ends in that moment. We state in the Nicene Creed, "I acknowledge one Baptism for the remission of sins." We don't get rebaptized because our Baptism has stopped working, as if we need to remind God to keep at it. Rather, we are baptized once, and that Baptism continues to work throughout the rest of our lives. It only takes a moment to be baptized, but once we are baptized, we never cease to be baptized.

4 Luther, *Luther's Works*, vol. 35 (Philadelphia: Fortress Press, 1960), 33–34.

That means that grace is always active. All the aspects of Baptism that we'll explore here will be at work as we continue to learn and grow as baptized children of God. We will always be sinners in this life, but that doesn't stop God from helping us to be more like the people He created us to be. This is why Luther says our Baptism is fulfilled at our death.[5] That is the point when the last vestiges of sin are wiped from our lives. "When the perishable puts on the imperishable, and the mortal puts on immortality, then shall come to pass the saying that is written: 'Death is swallowed up in victory'" (1 Corinthians 15:54). It is at this point we finally achieve the goal of Baptism—eternal life in Christ.

At a recent district pastors conference, I was asked to give a devotion on "Living in a Resurrection World." It's a topic that has a lot to do with Baptism since it is through Baptism that Christ's gift of eternal life explicitly becomes yours. Like Luther, whenever you are in doubt over what life holds or how you are going to make it through the day, you can always recall that you have been baptized. You may not know what next year, next month, or even tomorrow brings, but the end is not in doubt. Your Baptism stands as a sign and pledge to you that you have and will continue to receive everything God promises. That most assuredly means forgiveness, but it also means quite a bit more.

We'll be unpacking many of those benefits over the course of our study. For now, we simply remember that God has given us that promise and has bound Himself to us. He will never rescind that promise, for, as 1 John reminds us again, "He is faithful and just to forgive our sins and to cleanse us from all unrighteousness" (1:9). This is what He wants to do. He gives the Sacrament as a gift, and He enjoys giving it. Luther encourages you to be confident in your Baptism, for it is your blessed assurance that the resurrection will be yours as well. Whatever this life may throw at you, it will not be your end. It cannot be your end. You have been baptized.

5 See Luther, *Luther's Works*, vol. 36 (Philadelphia: Fortress Press, 1959), 69.

Hymn Connection

"God's Own Child, I Gladly Say It"

Text by Erdmann Neumeister

This hymn makes clear that Baptism gives many benefits beyond forgiveness. Protection from temptation, protection from Satan's wiles, reassurance of God's love, and proof of our place in eternal life are all found in Baptism. The hymn connects our lives now to our lives with Christ in eternity and explains that Baptism has an integral part to play in this connection. It does not tell us how all this comes to be true, but there is only so much one hymn can do all on its own.

In this case, it is enough to see how Luther's statement connecting death to Baptism can be found elsewhere if you look. In truth, it is because of Baptism that we rightly say Christians do not enter eternal life when they die. They have already died in Christ through Baptism, so they are already living their eternal life now. Their resurrection is assured.

In Romans 6:3–4, Paul tells us, "Do you not know that all of us who have been baptized into Christ Jesus were baptized into His death? We were buried therefore with Him by baptism into death, in order that, just as Christ was raised from the dead by the glory of the Father, we too might walk in newness of life." This is a pretty major piece of baptismal theology, for it tells us that our Baptism is truly linked to the death and resurrection of Christ. His life is ours through Baptism.

Usually when this passage is referenced, it is discussed in terms of how Baptism is our spiritual death. We "die" at the font so that we may be free from the condemnation of our sin. This idea is one Luther often brings up, such as in the Small Catechism, when he says, "What does such baptizing with water indicate?" Answer:

> It indicates that the Old Adam in us should by daily contrition and repentance be drowned and die with all sins and evil desires, and that a new man should daily emerge and arise to live before God in righteousness and purity forever. (Baptism, Fourth Part)

Your Baptism is like death and is just as serious. At the same time, this hymn and the statement from Luther about death as the fulfillment of Baptism also let us think about Baptism another way. If Baptism is like death, then that also means death is like Baptism. I'm simply flipping the words around, but Paul puts the two together, allowing you to truly take it either way. It may not sound like a big deal, but it should change your whole perception of death. The hymn reminds us of the end and how we will stand before the throne of the Lamb and celebrate the victory. Your Baptism is your assurance of a place in that victory celebration. That means just as death had no hold over Christ, death also has no hold over you. It is nothing to fear. If you weren't afraid to have some water poured over your head, then you truly have no reason to fear death either. Your death will end up being just as brief and worry-free as your Baptism.

Questions for Review

Luther took great comfort in the assurance given him in Baptism. Think back to some of the crises you've faced in life.

4. Would remembering your Baptism and what it means for your eternal life have changed how you reacted at the time?

5. Might it help you keep future crises in perspective?

As I write this, the world has been in the grip of the coronavirus pandemic. Many people have been terrified of catching the disease for fear of dying. Good stewardship of ourselves and our neighbors is certainly a concern and should be something we keep in mind. At the same time, a Christian who fears death is a Christian who has forgotten his Baptism. Your resurrection is already assured, and there is nothing in this life to fear. Whether the country suffers from a pandemic, a war, or an economic crisis, or whether the issue is something you struggle with personally, remember that you are baptized. God has already seen the end of whatever it is that you are facing, and He has seen that you will come through on the other side. He has promised.

UNIT 2

The Flood

As Old Testament events go, the flood isn't just one of the biggest events that relates to Baptism—it's one of the biggest events in history. Period. Luther makes it a central part of his Flood Prayer, which has continued to be a part of the Lutheran Rite of Baptism:

> Almighty and eternal God, according to Your strict judgment You condemned the unbelieving world through the flood, yet according to Your great mercy You preserved believing Noah and his family, eight souls in all.[6]

Obviously, both Baptism and the flood involve water. However, if the flood is going to tell us anything about Baptism, it has to do more than just have water. So let's take a look at the flood.

- Read Genesis 6:5–8.

1. According to God, what is the problem? What does He plan to do about it?

6 *LSB*, p. 268

2. **Why does sin grieve God?**

We don't know very much about the time after Adam and Eve. Genesis gives us a short story about Cain and Abel and then generally skips ahead to Noah. Things have gone downhill to the point that just about everyone in the world is only out for himself or herself. At this point, God seems ready to wipe everything out entirely. Luther states,

> [The evilness of man's thoughts] applies, therefore, not only to the sins before the Flood but to man's entire nature—to his heart, his reason, and his intellect, even when man feigns righteousness and wants to be most holy. This the Anabaptists do today when they get the idea into their heads that they can live without sin, and when they are intent on attaining what appear to be outstanding virtues. The rule is: When hearts are without the Holy Spirit, they do not only have no knowledge of God but even hate Him by nature. How can something that has its origin in a lack of knowledge of God and in a hatred of God be anything else than evil?[7]

It sounds pretty grim, but let's read a bit more.

- Read Genesis 6:9–7:5.

3. **What is the purpose of the flood?**

7 Luther, *Luther's Works*, vol. 2 (St. Louis: Concordia Publishing House, 1960), 43.

4. Whom is the flood directed against?

5. Why are Noah and his family spared from the flood?

6. Why do the plants and animals die in the flood too?

7. What about this passage reminds us of Baptism?

The flood God intends to send on the earth isn't from some desire to be cruel or vindictive. God does not delight in inflicting injury on anything in creation. He is the Creator who created this world out of love, not spite. Everything in creation was lovingly crafted to fit the niche He had specifically created for it. He is the master artist, and the universe is the canvas upon which He paints. It grieves Him when anything in His creation suffers. If we consider what it would be like if Leonardo da Vinci were forced to set fire to his Mona Lisa, we'd have some sense of what sending the flood on the world is like for God.

This is God's just and righteous judgment against sin and wickedness. Paul tells us in Romans 6:23, "For the wages of sin is death." Those who sin deserve to die. That isn't something we're comfortable hearing, and here we see God making good on that threat of punishment. Sin is the corruption of creation, destroying the good that God has made. If we consider da Vinci again, then it is like someone has come along and smeared tar across the whole canvas. The entire work is a loss except for one tiny corner da Vinci feels he can still salvage from the destruction. He could just throw the whole canvas away and start over. It would probably be easier. Instead, he chooses to put in the time and effort to save that tiny little piece because he cares about it and because he put in the work to craft it in the first place. Now the whole world is about to be washed away except for Noah's family in the ark.

It's worth noting that the flood is directed against the unrighteous people of the world, all but Noah and his family. Unfortunately, the plants and animals of the world are caught up in the same judgment. Genesis 3 shows us how mankind has an important role to play in God's creation. When men and women serve themselves instead of serving God and others, the whole order breaks down. Thorns and thistles grow where they shouldn't be growing because Adam doesn't know how to manage them anymore and his sinful nature doesn't want to manage them at all. Plants and animals are not rejecting their Creator, but they still die because of our sin.

Genesis 6:9 tells us Noah is a righteous man. Hebrews 11:7 makes clear that Noah became an "heir of the righteousness" because God warned him of what was coming, and Noah listened. Noah heeded the warning and trusted that God would save him and his family by the very means He outlined. Even though there was no evidence a flood such as God described would ever come, God's promise was enough for Noah. He trusted in that warning and promise, which is what made him and his family righteous out of all of the people on earth.

Looking at the design of Noah's ark, there are some elements (not just its size) that make it stand out from other boats. Most obvious is that there are no sails. It is not designed to catch the wind. It also does not have oars, a rudder, or anything else that might give it mobility. This boat will be designed for one simple purpose: to float. So not only is Noah building an absolutely massive boat, but he is also building a boat that is completely incapable of going anywhere. Luther remarks, "Surely, great was the faith of Noah that he was able to believe these words of God. I would certainly not have believed them."[8]

Peter describes Noah as the "herald of righteousness" (2 Peter 2:5). This suggests Noah did not shy away from telling others what God had told him in the hopes, perhaps, that they would repent and find salvation too. Unfortunately, no one else listened. God kindled faith in Noah's heart so that he was able to trust in God's warning and offer of salvation, even as the rest of the world rejected the warning and condemned themselves to death.

Luther writes,

> The Flood is truly death and the wrath of God; nevertheless, the believers are saved in the midst of the Flood. Thus death engulfs and swallows up the entire human race; for without distinction the wrath of God goes over the good and the evil, over the godly and the ungodly. The Flood that Noah experienced was not different from the one that the world experienced. The Red Sea, which both Pharaoh and Israel entered, was not different. Later on, however, the difference becomes apparent in this: those who believe are preserved in the very death to which they are subjected together with the ungodly, but the ungodly perish. Noah, accordingly, is preserved because he has the ark, that is, God's promise and Word, in which he is living; but the ungodly, who do not believe the

8 Luther, *Luther's Works*, vol. 2, 87.

Word, are left to their fate.[9]

The whole world is baptized, but Noah and his family are the only ones to be drawn back out of the water. That's why Luther says this in the Small Catechism: "How can water do such great things?" Answer:

"Certainly not just water, but the word of God in and with the water does these things, along with the faith which trusts this word of God in the water" (Baptism, Third Part). God's word made the water of the flood a destructive, world-changing event. But Noah trusted in God's promise, so the water didn't kill him like it did the rest of the world. God spoke, and Noah believed.

God's judgment rains down a number of times in the Old Testament. Several of these instances you may know well, such as the flood, when God sends fire down upon Sodom and Gomorrah for their blatant disregard for anyone but themselves, or when He sends the final plague on Egypt to wipe out the firstborn males of the land. In each case, God shows the extent to which He will destroy sin in the land. His judgment hits the land like a hammer, striking it until it shatters and the sin is finally put away or removed. However, in each case, those who trust in Him are saved from the devastation. Death falls all around, but those who look to Him for protection are kept safe.

Through the flood, God sought to wipe away the unrepentant sin from the land. The whole world experiences this washing of the water. The water is deadly and brings destruction everywhere, but not for Noah. Noah trusts in God, so the water has no judgment to give there. Where water brings death everywhere else, for Noah it brings new life and a new world to step out into. It is as fresh and pure as anything can be prior to the resurrection.

- Read 1 Peter 3:18–22.

---

9 Luther, *Luther's Works*, vol. 2, 153.

8. What did Noah receive through the waters of the flood?

The rest of life on earth died, but not Noah. In a figurative sense, Noah rose from the dead, much like Jesus would later do. This isn't the only place the Bible talks this way. I mentioned Hebrews 11:7 a few pages back. This passage describes exemplars of the faith, notably Noah and Abraham. The author of Hebrews tells us Abraham also received Isaac back from the dead when he was called upon to sacrifice his son. God meant what He said when He commanded Abraham to sacrifice His son, and Abraham listened and followed through until God stopped him. Noah is described as someone who, in reverent fear, built the ark to save his household from a threat he had no evidence would ever come. Both men trusted in God's promise and were saved from death by listening to Him. God is teaching us a bit about what Jesus would later demonstrate through His own death and resurrection. In the next unit, we'll look more at the implications of what Noah experienced:

> That water drowned everything that had life. Thus Baptism drowns everything that is carnal and natural; it makes spiritual men. But we take ship in the ark, which represents the Lord Christ, or the Christian Church, or the Gospel which Christ preaches, or the body of Christ to which we cling through faith; and we are saved, just as Noah was saved in the ark. Thus you see that the analogy summarizes what faith and the cross, life and death, are. Now where there are people who cling to Christ, there a Christian Church is sure to be. There everything that comes from Adam and is evil is drowned.[10]

Sin is judged, and all that remains is righteousness. The world is washed

10 Luther, *Luther's Works*, vol. 30 (St. Louis: Concordia Publishing House, 1967), 115–16.

clean, and the stain of sin is removed. Noah was saved from death because he trusted in God to save him. God provided the means of escaping the devastation. By trusting that God would uphold His promise, Noah lives through the punishment of death that was dealt out to the whole world and comes out on the other side unscathed.

Further in Depth

The flood already shows us some very important connections to Baptism. We'll continue looking at themes that will reinforce what we have already seen here, but some of those themes are already coming out quite strongly. Noah's trust in God turned aside the worldwide destruction, a tiny bubble of life in a world covered in watery death.

While everything we've looked at so far broadens our understanding of what Baptism does for us now, there are also some important things to remember here and as we continue through our study of baptismal themes in the Old Testament. The first is that the flood may tell us about Baptism, but the flood is not actually Baptism. This is one of those statements I'll make that may sound obvious, but it bears consideration. God did send the flood to wipe out the unrighteous people across the land. God granted Noah the power to trust His ominous pronouncement of the impending flood. Noah built the ark, gathered his family and the animals, and was saved, just as God promised. The rest of the world perished in its sin.

This might suggest that Noah is now free from sin since he survived the flood that came to wipe sin away from creation. But Noah is still very much a sinner. He still grows old and dies, just like anyone else. The flood has much to teach us about Baptism. It shows us the extent to which God will go to wipe out sin. It shows us how even in an event that wipes out quite literally everyone else on the planet, God can and will save those who trust in Him. However, God never promises He will wipe away Noah's sin with the flood. That isn't what the flood was ever meant to do.

Back at the beginning of the unit, we saw how Luther connected the flood to Baptism. Just as foreshadowing in a book is intended to prepare you for when the real event comes, the flood prepares us for Baptism. The flood could never serve the purpose of Baptism, for full and complete salvation can only be found in Christ. Until the coming of Christ, no event in history has the power to offer anything more than temporary safety. The Early Church theologian Tertullian wrote quite a bit on Baptism. He speaks to this as well:

> For just as, after the waters of the deluge, by which the old iniquity was purged—after the baptism, so to say, of the world—a *dove* was the herald which announced to the earth the assuagement of celestial wrath, when she had been sent her way out of the ark, and had returned with the olive-branch, a sign which even among the nations is the fore-token of *peace;* so by the self-same law of heavenly effect, to earth—that is, to our flesh—as it emerges from the font, after its old sins, flies the *dove* of the Holy Spirit, bringing us the peace of God, sent out from the heavens, where is the Church, the typified ark. But the world returned unto sin; in which point baptism would ill be compared to the deluge. And so it is destined to fire; just as the man too is, who after baptism renews his sins: so that this also ought to be accepted as a sign for our admonition.[11]

Tertullian says a lot about the Holy Spirit here. We'll get to Him a bit later in our study. Right now we are more interested in how Tertullian points out that the world returned to sin. If we were to continue reading Genesis, we'd see that it is not all that long after Noah leaves the ark and his family resettles the land that we have the tower of Babel incident. God does

11 Tertullian, "On Baptism," in *The Ante-Nicene Fathers: The Writings of the Fathers down to AD 32*, vol. 3 (Grand Rapids, MI: Eerdmans, 1957), 673.

not wipe out the people here, but He does take pretty drastic action to thwart their sinful endeavors.

The flood has come and gone for Noah. Many unbelievers were wiped out, but sin is not gone for good. Not yet. For that to happen, God needs to do something even bigger and more sweeping. There are many other elements that need to come together to make that possible. This is why the flood and every other work God does on behalf of His people ultimately points us to Christ. He will be the one to bring all this together and give it purpose.

Hymn Connection

"Great Is Thy Faithfulness"

Text by Thomas O. Chisholm

The lyrics to this hymn do not specifically refer to the flood or to the beginning of creation. What they do refer to is the long-standing work of God in the midst of creation. Whether during the flood or any other disaster, God still keeps His promises. Creation itself bears witness to how God provides for His faithful people even when it looks like nothing could possibly save them. The time Noah spent building the ark, surviving the storm, and then waiting for the waters to subside is a testimony to how God keeps them safe in both the short term and over the long haul.

Questions for Review

9. What does God say about the lengths He will go to in order to wipe out sin?

10. Think about Noah as he hears God tell him to build an ark for the upcoming disaster. If you had been in his position, how do you think you would have responded?

11. Consider also the nature of the flood. If God can provide for Noah in the midst of a disaster that wipes out all that moves on the ground, is there truly anything He can't protect you from?

God's devastation of all that lived on the dry land is complete and total. This already tells us something about how God views sin. No amount of sin can be tolerated in God's good creation. Noah does not quite arrive in a completely new and sinless world, for he himself still has sin. However, this still shows us something about what God will do later when it is time to fully inaugurate God's new world. As for our response to God's declaration, it's hard to see how any of us would take such a statement very seriously. Even Luther admits such an announcement is beyond belief. The fact that Noah hears and believes is an expression of exactly how faith works. In spite of the lack of immediate evidence, God grants us the ability to trust Him and find salvation. Truly, if God can save Noah from a disaster like this, there is nothing God cannot save you from.

UNIT 3

Creation

Noah's experience of the flood is quite profound. Life on earth is washed away, but Noah and his family remain. Judgment falls, but they are spared. Noah gets his life back. That, all by itself, tells us something about what God will do later through water and His Word. But as far back in history as the flood was, it was already looking further back to events that had come before it. Let's take a look.

- Read Genesis 1:1–2:3.

1. What is the first thing to exist in all creation?

2. What significant things are taking place on the second and third days?

3. What are the parameters God uses in His creation of man?

4. What event completes God's creative work?

5. Which persons of the Trinity are involved in creation?

The whole work of creation is something we learn about as Christians, but rarely do we dig into some of the details that God has hidden there. Creation is very much a trinitarian work. Right from the very beginning, the triune God is fully involved in His new creation. We typically think of light as the first thing God makes, and it is certainly the highlight of the first day, but we see the Spirit hovering over this formless ball of water, the first thing God makes and the substance He uses to build the rest of our world. The Father oversees all this activity. But rather than molding the world with His hands, building and shaping every rock and tree as one might make a diorama, the Father simply speaks. The Gospel of John tells us this is where we find the Son, the Word by whom all things were made. The Father speaks, and that message, that Word, is Christ Himself. This work of the Trinity will be an important connection later as we examine Baptism. For now, it tells us how involved each person is in the work of creation.

The third day brings plants into God's creation, but before that, God divides the waters into those above and those below. Already we are setting the stage for what we'll see later in the flood. Scripture doesn't tell us what the purpose of this division is. It tells us simply that God determined that it needed to happen to make the world habitable.

The creation of Adam and Eve is an event that has been the focus of a great many theological debates. God creates man "in His own image" (Genesis 1:27). The word *image* is not meant in a physical sense here but in a spiritual and metaphorical sense. As God picks up a clump of earth and molds the first man, He creates that man to be in a relationship with Him. For that to happen, that man must be perfect, for God's presence cannot allow sin without destroying it utterly. As a perfect man, Adam trusts God implicitly and thus carries God's own righteousness. Because Adam is perfect, there is nothing broken in him that could lead to his body's breakdown and eventual death. Adam is in the image of God because he reflects God's love right back to Him.

When Adam sins, he loses that image because he is no longer able to reflect God's love back to Him. Adam is filled with love for himself instead of love for others. With that sin, God's created order breaks down, and now everything is subject to decay, disorder, and death. Adam was created in the image of God, but he lost it through his own sinful choice. Now, if Adam is to be restored to the image he was created to have, God must bring about that restoration.

Before Adam's sin, God completes His work by resting on the seventh day and marking it as a holy day of rest. The whole world falls into this system of seven days making up a week and then repeating. God created the world to work that way, and we all naturally fall into that rhythm.

Before we continue looking at creation, let's put some pieces together.

- Read Genesis 9:7–17.

6. **What are the terms of the covenant God establishes with Noah?**

7. **Who is the rainbow for? What is its purpose?**

8. **What is the command God gives Noah and his family?**

In order to answer the questions, we must put ourselves in the place of Noah. He climbs into the ark with his family and all the animals. God shuts the door. Then it starts to rain. The people die. The animals and plants die. Dry land disappears. The sun, moon, and stars disappear. Genesis 7:11 tells us, "On that day all the fountains of the great deep burst forth, and the windows of the heavens were opened." The waters God had separated on the third day come together again. Under forty days of rain, God rewinds the days of creation as even light is more or less erased under the dark storm clouds.

When the rain finally ceases, Noah looks out over the side of the ark and sees nothing but water stretching unbroken to the horizon in every direction. It is almost as if he is there at the very beginning of creation where nothing exists but the water God will use to build the rest of the world. Then, slowly, all the things God made start to return. The dark, angry storm clouds calm and allow light to trickle through. Eventually, they part, and the heavenly bodies are visible in the sky. Dry land appears, and the ark finally comes to rest. Then the world is filled once more with plants, animals, and people.

God calls to mind the command He gave Adam and Eve back in Genesis 1:28: “Be fruitful and multiply and fill the earth and subdue it, and have dominion over the fish of the sea and over the birds of the heavens and over every living thing that moves on the earth.” Noah walks out of the ark into a world that closely resembles the world of Genesis 1. It is as if God had wound back time and reset the world through the flood. The unrighteous people have been washed away, and the world has been made clean once more.

Sin is not completely gone, but God tells us something about what He does with water. The world is re-created through the flood. Noah trusted in God, and his trust was not in vain. Like Abraham later on, Noah trusted and was counted as righteous because he was saved from judgment. The flood waters came in judgment, but Noah was saved and not destroyed. Noah need never face this kind of judgment again, for he is already righteous. God puts the rainbow in the sky, not for Noah but for Himself. From this time forward, whenever God looks down at Noah, He'll see the rainbow and remember Noah has already been judged and found innocent.

In the same way, our Baptism protects us and is a constant reminder to God that we have already been washed clean and made righteous. We trust in God and come to the font, knowing that He'll wash our sins away and that our trust is not in vain. It also means we have been re-created and restored to our original state of righteousness in the eyes of God. We have been given the image of God once more. We'll take a closer look at what that means in the next unit.

For now, let's back up a bit and look at one more section.

- Read Genesis 7:6–8:12.

9. What are the different time frames listed here? Are those times significant? If so, how?

10. What, if anything, is significant about the creatures that show up in this section of text?

Things that get repeated in various places in Scripture are not always related. However, when you see something show up more than once, such as the number *7*, it's worth at least investigating to see if they are connected somehow. This sort of repetition isn't usually something you want to put too much weight on unless the text specifically says why it's important, but it often works as circumstantial evidence. Enough circumstantial evidence eventually adds up to a pretty strong connection. I'm not going to unpack all these things at this point because we need to explore some other ideas first before these puzzle pieces will fit. But we need to at least mark them down so we remember where they came from.

First is the number *7*. This should already be making us think of creation, and rightly so. We've already seen how the flood is a restoration of God's initial work in creation. However, Genesis 7:10 says the rain began not on the seventh day but *after* the seventh day. That makes the number not *7*, but *7 + 1*, or *8*. This number will actually show up more than once in Scripture and will play a rather important role in our understanding of Baptism. The number *7* also shows up in chapter 8 as Noah tests things with some birds to see if life has returned to earth. Perhaps a reinforcement of the creation theme as God is busy restoring the world as the waters subside.

The number *40* also shows up here a couple times. It shows up in Genesis 7:17 and then again in 8:6. Genesis 8:6 suggests a time of waiting—forty days that Noah has been waiting for things to begin to return to normal. Genesis 7:17 tells us the rain fell for forty days. God inflicted His wrath against sin on the world for forty days. In either case, we see the number *40* show up in Scripture in a couple of other significant places, such as the number of days Jesus spent in the wilderness being tempted after His Baptism. We also see it as the number of years the Israelites spent in the wilderness before entering the Promised Land. Both of these will come up again in our study.

Finally, the dove comes into play. Doves don't show up much in Scripture. The most noteworthy place is, of course, Jesus' own Baptism. This also suggests something important and worth looking into. All these pieces have a common thread: Baptism. None of them are enough to base a lot on all by themselves, but looking at how and where they connect will add further weight to the idea that everything going on back here with creation and the flood is really meant to tell us about what God will be doing later in Baptism.

Further in Depth

Studying the flood and creation gives us the opportunity to talk about the "now/not yet" concept that runs through the New Testament. As Jesus says in John 15, He and His disciples are not of the world. We are always looking for the new creation that is to come when He returns in glory. We know at that point that sin will be wiped away forever and we will enjoy perfect peace. That peace can't exist in this world because we and the world are still tainted by sin.

The perfect joy and peace that awaits us with the return of Christ and the resurrection of all flesh is something all Christians eagerly look forward to. At the end of Revelation, Jesus says, "Surely I am coming soon." John and the whole Church reply, "Amen. Come, Lord Jesus!" (22:20). We constantly pray for Christ to return and bring a full and final end to sin, death, and Satan because they still torment God's people.

Though we are waiting for the day when sin will be completely gone, we also know Christ has already died for our sins and forgives those sins now. Luther speaks to this in his discussion of Confession in the Small Catechism:

> What is Confession? Confession has two parts. First, that we confess our sins, and second, that we receive absolution, that is forgiveness, from the pastor as from God Himself, not doubting, but firmly believing that by it our sins are forgiven before God in heaven. (Confession, "What is Confession?")

We are looking for what God has promised to do for us in the future, but God is also already at work in the world now. Even though we are still living with sin in our lives because Christ hasn't returned, we are already seen as sinless by Him because the sins we have are forgiven.

This idea extends to just about every other aspect of our lives, as well as the lives of those who have come before us. Baptism works similarly here. As we look back to Noah, we can see how the flood showed him a bit of what was to come. The flood looked forward to a washing that would cleanse not just the surface but the inside as well, namely Baptism. Though the Sacrament of Baptism did not exist in Noah's day, God was still at work in his life. Noah still saw God's salvation as He saved him from physical death and still acknowledged him as righteous.

Noah stepped out of the ark into a world that resembled the world God had first created, but it still bore the taint of sin. Noah looked forward to a world that would truly be free of sin. But even with the flood, it had not arrived yet. Baptism would do more than the flood did since it brings spiritual cleansing, but it still doesn't solve the problem of sin in the world completely either. Luther also says of Baptism in the Small Catechism,

> What does such baptizing with water indicate? It indicates that the Old Adam in us should by daily contrition and repentance be drowned and die with all sins and evil desires, and that a new man should daily emerge and arise to live before God in righteousness and purity forever. (Baptism, Fourth Part)

Hymn Connection

"Joyful, Joyful We Adore Thee"

Text by Henry Van Dyke

Psalm 8:3–4 says, "When I look at Your heavens, the work of Your fingers, the moon and the stars, which You have set in place, what is man that You are mindful of him, and the son of man that You care for him?" Psalm 19:1–2 says, "The heavens declare the glory of God, and the sky above proclaims His handiwork. Day to day pours out speech, and night to night reveals knowledge." In both cases, the psalmist reflects on the wonders of creation. God has made the world and everything in it. Everything He makes reflects who He is and bears His stamp. Adam and Eve may not have realized how wondrous the world was when they took their first steps in the Garden of Eden, but they probably thought about it quite a bit after they were sent out from it. The world still proclaimed the glory of its Creator to the best of its ability, but it had a much more difficult time doing so.

Noah glimpses this as he steps out of the ark, and for the moment, everything looks pristine. The world is as close to perfection as creation can be with sin still running through it. The joy that filled creation as God's creatures entered into it once more, having survived their baptismal flood, was assuredly a thing to behold. Noah and all creation now bore witness to a mighty act of God and proof that He saves His people even when judgment falls on the entire rest of the world. Noah and all living things would look in awe at the rainbow that filled the skies and know with certainty they had received God's great mercy.

Questions for Review

11. As you're going about your life over the week, take a moment to consider some of the everyday things you come across. What would they be like if you were able to take them back to the garden before the fall into sin?

12. Would they work or act differently? If so, how? Consider how much your life would change if everything around you worked perfectly like it would have in the garden.

We tend to think of many things as normal simply because they happen all the time. Cats scratch people. Dogs bite. Gusting storms knock down tree limbs that damage power lines and houses. Spiders scare people. Cars break down. All these issues are a part of the fallen world. Cats, dogs, spiders, and winds all existed in the garden, yet they did none of those things. Cars, perhaps, also would have existed in time but never would have broken down. That makes all those problems very abnormal, at least as God sees them. Every aspect of this world is tainted by sin, but we rarely think about it because that's the only world we know. Nearly everything in the world would operate very, very differently if sin were no longer a factor. We don't know exactly what life in God's new creation will look like, but we do know it will have the same kind of perfection Adam and Eve knew before sin came into the world. The few glimpses we are given in Scripture of the new creation show a world that reflects that same kind of pristine life that once existed so long ago.

UNIT 4

The Image of God

The image of God isn't just a matter of who you are but also what you do. Adam and Eve were created in God's own righteousness, which meant they had jobs to do in the world where God had placed them. God has already given them a command in Genesis 1:28. Let's take a look again.

- Read Genesis 1:26–30.

1. What are Adam and Eve supposed to do?

Aside from being fruitful and multiplying, Adam and Eve were supposed to manage the world God had given them. This doesn't mean God had abandoned His supervision of the world. It was more like He involved Adam and Eve in His work. God built the rules for how the world would work. He allowed Adam and Eve to manage things within that system. Luther says a bit more:

> Here [in Gen. 1:26] the rule is assigned to the most beautiful creature, who knows God and is the image of God, in whom the similitude of the divinc nature shines forth through his enlightened reason, through his justice and his wisdom. Adam and Eve become the rulers of the earth, the sea, and the

> air. . . . Adam and Eve heard the words with their ears when God said: "Have dominion." Therefore the naked human being—without weapons and walls, even without any clothing, solely in his bare flesh—was given the rule over all birds, wild beasts, and fish.[12]

Adam and Eve carry the authority of the Creator as they tend to the world around them. God makes the flowers grow, but Adam and Eve are given the authority to tell them where to grow. But with the loss of the image of God, this job becomes more difficult. Let's take a look at what dominion looks like now.

- Read Genesis 3:17–19.

2. What does this dominion look like in a fallen world?

Adam and Eve still have the job, but nothing works like it is intended to anymore. Where once they might have laid out orderly orchards and flower beds and known everything would grow exactly where they wanted, now the connection between God and creation, which flows through mankind, is broken, and creation grows wild and unmanaged.

In general, Baptism is the means by which God returns us to that original image and righteousness we once had, but Scripture also tells us more about how important Baptism is to this restoration. Now let's look at how God starts to bring us back into that position:

- Read 1 Samuel 16:1–13.

---

12 Luther, *Luther's Works*, vol. 1 (St. Louis: Concordia Publishing House, 1958), 66.

3. **Who receives the anointing here?**

4. **What is the purpose of the anointing?**

Samuel takes the oil and pours it on the head of David, and now David is marked as king over Israel. Saul had initially been chosen to be the first king of Israel. Unfortunately, it didn't take Saul long to follow his own path. He stopped listening to God and opted instead to do things his own way. Saul disqualified himself from the position of king.

So God chooses David to replace him. David is anointed here, announcing that God has chosen him and will establish him as king. David lives as a shepherd now and has very little experience in leading armies or ruling a nation, so God gives him time to learn the ropes before he takes on the job. He may not be officially ruling yet, but God has named him king, so it is a foregone conclusion that it will come to pass. Soon, Saul will be removed and David will take his place on the throne as king. It may seem rather strange to use oil to mark a king, but oil has a very special purpose in the life of God's people.

- Read Exodus 30:22–33.

5. **What does God say is the purpose of this oil?**

6. **What does it mean to be made holy?**

7. **Why couldn't anyone else use this oil?**

The anointing oil is used for pouring over many things. Most of the items used for ritual service to God, such as the furnishings of the tabernacle and all the utensils, are anointed with this oil. This marks them as holy—given to and claimed by God. This is why God alone uses the oil. He doesn't want anyone else to be confused about what its purpose is. The things (or people) anointed with this oil are His and will always be His. They are not to be used for mundane purposes anymore.

In this particular case, Aaron and his sons are being anointed. We'll look a bit more at them in the next unit. For now, we can see the purpose here. Whatever Aaron might have been before, now he is anointed and given to God to be put to work in His service to bring His grace to the people. Aaron is different than the man he was before. He is no longer his own person. He must think and act like a representative of God and know that the things he does, whether good or bad, will reflect on God as well.

In that way, Aaron was reflecting God's own Son, Jesus Christ. In His Baptism, Jesus was anointed with the Holy Spirit, set apart as God's perfect representative. "He is the radiance of the glory of God and the exact imprint of His nature, and He upholds the universe by the word of His power" (Hebrews 1:3). Or as Jesus said about His ministry, "Do you not believe that I am in the Father and the Father is in Me? The words that I say to you I do not speak on My own authority, but the Father who dwells in Me does His works" (John 14:10).

There's a reason the Church has always referred to the Sacrament as "Holy Baptism." When Jesus tells His disciples to baptize "in the name of the Father and of the Son and of the Holy Spirit" (Matthew 28:19), it tells us that God is, in essence, putting His stamp of ownership on that person baptized, just as the oil of anointing did in the days of the Israelites.

To be baptized, then, is to be restored to the original state of kingship mankind was meant to have—the same kingship Adam had. Luther says,

> And again, the situation of Adam, as the initiator of sin, was worse than ours, if we appraise it correctly. Where we work hard, each one in his own station, Adam was compelled to exert himself in the hard work of the household, of the state, and of the church all by himself. As long as he lived, he alone held all these positions among his descendants. He supported his family, ruled it, and trained it in godliness; he was father, king, and priest. And experience teaches how each one of these positions abounds in grief and dangers.[13]

In the Old Testament, kings were made by anointing. Jesus was made King of kings and Lord of lords at His Baptism when He was anointed with the Holy Spirit. New Testament kings are made by Baptism. Adam and Eve were to have dominion over the world, serving as king and queen under the King of kings. This was the position and duty they gave up when they tried to go beyond their creaturely limitations and have something more. Now God restores us to that role and gives us the ability to look beyond ourselves to the world around us and see how it is ours to care for and protect. Let's look at the other two classes of people who receive anointing and how they relate to us.

13 Luther, *Luther's Works*, vol. 1, 213–14.

As we saw, anointing was God's way of showing the world what was His. The role of king was one Adam and Eve had from the very beginning, but kings aren't the only ones who are anointed. Let's go back and take another look at Aaron.

- Read Leviticus 8:1–10, 30–36.

8. What is the purpose of the anointing?

9. Why does Aaron receive this anointing?

10. What is the time frame over which this ordination takes place?

11. What is significant about this time frame?

This is quite an involved chapter. Aaron puts on all the vestments of priesthood, and Moses offers sacrifices on Aaron's behalf. The anointing seen here accomplishes the same thing for Aaron as we learned it did for King David. In this case, God is not claiming Aaron as a king but as a priest. Aaron will have a special role in the work of God's grace and forgiveness.

Aaron will act as the go-between, speaking God's words of forgiveness to the people and offering their gifts back to Him.

Earlier in this unit, we saw Luther comment on how Adam was both a king and a priest. Adam was meant to order and organize creation, but he was also meant to be the connecting point between God and the rest of the world. As he turned his attention on himself and not on God or the world, he gave up this role as well. Now this connection is severed and the world is full of sin. For God to exist in a sinful world without destroying it outright, He must cleanse pieces of it so He can be here without hurting us. This is why the tabernacle and all its furnishings are anointed and consecrated to God's service. They won't be sullied by mundane use that might prevent them from serving as tools for God's grace. Aaron, too, is anointed and claimed by God. He is not to sully himself with worldly things anymore. If he is too corrupted by worldly sins that he no longer sees his position as important, then God's people lose that connection to their Creator.

In 1 Peter 2:5, Peter declares that the Church is "a spiritual house, to be a holy priesthood, to offer spiritual sacrifices acceptable to God through Jesus Christ." He echoes the declaration God made to the Israelites and now applies it to us. What Aaron does and what Adam was meant to do was intended to be something the whole nation participated in. What Aaron did for the Israelites was something all the Israelites were supposed to be doing for the rest of the world. They were supposed to be bringing the concerns of the world to God and sharing what God says about those things. They fell into heathen religions and gave up that role. The holy priesthood is critical to the working of God's grace and for the care of the people. So God removed the Israelites as His people and found a new group of people to fill the role: the Church.

The ordination of Aaron takes place over seven days, and he begins his service on the eighth. This number should make us think of the days of creation. God takes seven days to complete the work of creation. In that work of creation, Adam and Eve are made in the image of God. With the loss of the image of God, God anoints Aaron and, in a sense, re-creates him by sending him through that creation all over again. This is similar to the sense we get from Noah and the flood as well. Aaron is put back into the role Adam once had. Luther says further,

> After God has given man the administration of government and of the home, has set him up as king of the creatures, and has added the tree of life as a safeguard for preserving this physical life, He now builds him, as it were, a temple that he may worship Him and thank the God who has so kindly bestowed all these things on him. Today in our churches we have an altar for the administration of the Eucharist, and we have platforms or pulpits for teaching the people. These objects were built not only to meet a need but also to create a solemn atmosphere. But this tree of the knowledge of good and evil was Adam's church, altar, and pulpit. Here he was to yield to God the obedience he owed, give recognition to the Word and will of God, give thanks to God, and call upon God for aid against temptation.[14]

Aaron is made a priest again through this anointing, which prefigures Jesus' Baptism, when He was anointed as our High Priest. God achieves the same result in us through Holy Baptism. We, too, are brought back into the priesthood and given the duty of being the go-between for God and the rest of the world.

The anointing of priests and kings is significant all on its own, but those are not the only people God anoints.

- Read 1 Kings 19:9–18.

---

14 Luther, *Luther's Works*, vol. 1, 94–95.

12. Who does God direct Elijah to anoint? What roles do they serve?

We've seen kings anointed already. So, it is no surprise that Elijah would be directed to anoint kings here. However, prophets are new to us. As theirs is another position that's important to the functioning of God's people, it shouldn't surprise us that prophets would be ordained as well. But what is it that makes someone a prophet? Let's take a look.

- Read Deuteronomy 18:15–22.

13. How would you know if someone is a prophet?

14. What is prophecy?

15. Are there prophets in the world today?

Looking back on the life of Moses and of the prophets that will come after him, God describes what makes someone a prophet. We tend to think of prophecy as just telling the future, but there's a subtle distinction here. Prophets aren't really interested in telling the future. They are there to proclaim God's Word. Because the messages proclaimed by God's prophets are His, they must come to pass. Whether the Word to be proclaimed is one of salvation or judgment, the prophet's job is the same.

The list of those individuals God called specifically to be prophets ended with John the Baptist. When Jesus was anointed with the Holy Spirit in His Baptism, Jesus took His place as prophet supreme. Though the biblical role of prophet has ended, Christians are still called to be prophets in their lives today. With the completion of Scripture, there is nothing new to be revealed to God's people before Christ returns. In that sense, prophets are no longer necessary. However, as Christians, we are still called to proclaim the Word God has revealed. God told us much about the future regarding the new creation and the work He has yet to complete. He has promised it to His people, and His promise will be fulfilled. That means we still have work to do proclaiming what God says about life in the present day and about what is yet to come in the future.

You might wonder why proclaiming the Word is part of the image of God, but Adam's first failure was not in eating the fruit. He failed to proclaim God's Word to defend Eve from Satan. He failed in his duty as prophet, and thus, even though Eve eats the fruit first, the fault lies with Adam. This is why, with one exception, Scripture puts the blame for the fall of the world into sin squarely on him. Thus, anointing and Baptism seek to restore us to that duty and give us the knowledge of God needed to speak His will and Word into the sinful and unbelieving world.

Further in Depth

In Matthew 12:39–41, Jesus tells the Pharisees and scribes, "An evil and adulterous generation seeks for a sign, but no sign will be given to it except the sign of the prophet Jonah. For just as Jonah was three days and three nights in the belly of the great fish, so will the Son of Man be three days and three nights in the heart of the earth. The men of Nineveh will rise up at the judgment with this generation and condemn it, for they repented at the preaching of Jonah, and behold, something greater than Jonah is here." Jesus explains that Jonah's time in the belly of the fish relates to Christ's own death and resurrection.

Jonah's time in the fish certainly looks baptismal. After all, you've got someone being saved from death and a whole lot of water. Jesus' statement that it relates to His death and resurrection helps too, but taking a look at the story itself is the best way to see what Jonah's time in the fish is really all about.

If you take the time to read through the Book of Jonah—it's only four chapters, so it won't take you long—you'll probably remember a lot of the basic elements of the story. There's Jonah the prophet. There's God's command to Jonah to go preach to Nineveh. There's Jonah literally running away from God at every opportunity. God saves Jonah from drowning. Jonah goes to Nineveh finally and then has his pity party overlooking the city.

Jonah's time in the fish looks very baptismal. God saves Jonah from death. And yet salvation isn't really the point of the fish. Jonah *is* saved, true. But Jonah isn't saved so he can run off and do whatever he wants. Jonah is saved *so he can be a prophet.* God gave Jonah a job at the very beginning of the book. That hasn't changed. The job still needs to be done. God saves Jonah so that he may carry out the task given to him: to proclaim His will to a pagan people. In this way, Jonah's salvation by the fish is very baptismal.

Looking at these different roles, we are led to the question of how we are restored to these roles. Certainly, this takes place in Baptism, but the question is *why*. Why does Baptism bring us back to these roles we were created to have?

To answer that, we remember what the roles of prophet, priest, and king all relate to: the image of God. We're again talking about creation, about the world as God originally made it. The first person who bore the image of God was Adam. Adam perfectly carried out all these roles, right up until he didn't. When he sinned, he abdicated these responsibilities, and creation became subject to disorder and death as a result.

In Romans 5, Paul tells us Adam's life was pointing ahead to Jesus. We often refer to Jesus as the Second Adam. Jesus relives Adam's life in many ways, but where Adam fell to temptation and brought sin into the world, Jesus would resist temptation and bring life. Jesus resists Satan at the beginning of His ministry. Jesus follows His Father's will perfectly. Again, we see those echoes of creation. Again, Jesus is busy resetting things to the way they were created to be. Jesus carries out the roles of prophet, priest, and king that Adam was meant to fill. Where Adam failed, Jesus will succeed.

Our Baptism restores us to that state of righteousness the world once had—a world only made possible through the life of Christ. He continues to carry out those roles in His perfect and sinless humanity. Our lives as prophets, priests, and kings or queens are a reflection of His. Our work in those roles is only possible because He makes it so by bringing us back to the righteousness we were meant to have.

Baptism restores our role in the world and then directs and empowers us to carry out that role.

Hymn Connection

"God of the Prophets, Bless the Prophets' Sons"

Text by Denis Wortman

This hymn is often used at ordinations and installations. It expresses some of the aspects of what God calls Christians to do. Though it doesn't explicitly refer to Baptism, it brings in the three different vocations that God anoints throughout Scripture together in one hymn. You may have sung this hymn before without really thinking about how this all comes to be. Now that we have looked at anointing and its connection to Baptism, you can see how God has made all this—not just for pastors, but for all Christians.

Questions for Review

16. As you think about your own vocation as a baptized prophet, priest, and king or queen, what does all that mean for how you interact with those outside the Church?

Kings and queens are tasked with helping the world to flourish by maintaining order and protecting it. That goes for not just the people inhabiting the world but also for the rest of it, for it was all created by God. Kings and queens care for the world, but even they need the guidance and support of their Creator. Priests hear the concerns of the world. So priests take the problems of the world to Him directly, asking Him to intervene in grace and mercy.

All this means there's quite a lot for baptized Christians to do. There is no sense in sitting around passively waiting for God to do things, for He has sent us to be His representatives and to love and care for His creation with our own two hands.

UNIT 5

CIRCUMCISION

Some of the major topics we've already touched on lead us to a new idea that comes into play when we talk about Baptism. To get a better feel for this new idea, let's take a look at another baptismal topic.

- Read Genesis 17:1–14.

1. What are the conditions of the covenant God establishes with Abraham?

2. What does Abraham receive in this covenant?

3. What is the significance of the time God requires for the covenant?

Despite the rather short passage, the connection between the covenant of circumcision and the Sacrament of Baptism is quite strong. Here God is claiming Abraham and his descendants as His people. Circumcision will be the mark by which the males will be known as the people of God. Their wives and daughters are even included in this covenant through the circumcision of the males. They are made different and distinct in this way. This is much the same idea as we saw back with anointing something or someone with the oil to make them holy and dedicated to God.

God is formalizing a relationship with Abraham and his descendants here. The people of the covenant will forever know they are God's people and that He is at work on their behalf. Should they reject the covenant, then they reject God. But unless that happens, they will always be His, no matter what else should befall them.

The time frame is also important here. A male child is to be circumcised when he is eight days old. While many theologians work out a defense of infant Baptism from the New Testament, the roots of this theology can be found right here. God claims a child only eight days old as His own. He doesn't simply offer it as an option or make suggestions here. He demands that it be done on the eighth day. God sees how necessary it is for His promise to come to each of us, even tiny babies. Circumcision is a command, just as Baptism is. However, it is a command that is tied to the promise of grace. God grants that promise of grace to all, even and especially to those who cannot even comprehend the magnitude of what they are receiving.

Modern medicine has found an interesting fact about circumcision in that the level of vitamin K that is necessary for blood clotting is not adequate to prevent a child from bleeding out during circumcision until he is at least eight days old.[15] Thus, circumcising a child before the eighth day

15 With modern medical advances and the vitamin K shot given to most newborns, baby boys can now be safely circumcised shortly after birth.

could have serious consequences. So there is not only a spiritual component to circumcision but also a physical one.

In this case, one who is circumcised becomes a child of the same promise made to Abraham. This promise looks ahead to what God will later say as He declares the Israelites to be "a people holy to the LORD your God, as He promised" (Deuteronomy 26:19). He also tells them, "You shall be to Me a kingdom of priests and a holy nation" (Exodus 19:6). When God speaks to Abraham, He tells him he will be "the father of a multitude of nations" (Genesis 17:4). Now God carries the covenant with Abraham further and tells the Israelites exactly what it means to be His people. They are His. They are holy.

Looking back at Aaron's ordination, there's a similar time frame at work. His ordination takes place over seven days. For those seven days, he's confined to the tabernacle as he waits for the rite to be completed. It is only on the eighth day that he actually begins his work as high priest over Israel.

Both circumcision and the ordination of the first high priest bring about a transformative change in the life of God's people. Each of them is taken from the people they were—people with no connection to God, no relationship with Him, and no ability to carry out the roles they were created to have—and each is made into someone new. Through circumcision, each Israelite becomes a child of the covenant and promise God made. Each becomes a recipient of everything God declared would be given to His people. Aaron becomes a priest again, with the privilege of coming into God's presence and of communicating the cares of creation to Him.

In Unit 3, I discussed how the eighth day on which it begins to rain in Noah's day might be an important connection later. Here we have found similar ideas coming together around the theme of Baptism. As with Aaron, there is a seven-day waiting period, then the big event actually commences. It might appear there's a difference in the activity since the eighth day is when Aaron begins working, and it is the eighth day when Noah is finally finished working, but this would be looking at it from the wrong direction. In both cases, the eighth day is when God begins working in earnest. Judgment for the world and salvation for Noah both enter on this day, while God also establishes a more intimate and interactive relationship with His people through Aaron.

Each of these looks to a restoration of creation, which would be suggested by the number *7*, but then looks beyond it to something new. Let's explore this idea a bit more.

- Read Romans 6:1–11.

4. What does Paul mean by "newness of life" (v. 4)?

5. According to Paul, what role does Baptism play in our lives?

Paul looks back on events such as circumcision to show us how sinners can be bound to God through the establishment of His covenantal promise. Had God not declared the significance of circumcision, the act would have meant nothing. But because of His promise, circumcision becomes the outward mark indicating that this Israelite belongs to God and is one of His people. Now Baptism carries on the same work in our lives by joining us to the life of Christ. We are baptized into the life of Christ. His death is our death through Baptism, so His resurrection will be ours as well.

Jesus Himself was circumcised in accordance with the command God gave to Abraham. He will go on to be baptized and, in so doing, bring together the Old Testament and the New Testament in His own life. Those who were circumcised were looking forward to the point when Jesus brings something new and greater into the world. He is the fulfillment of everything that has come before, so all believers in the Old Testament age are brought into the same promises we are because all are joined to the life of Christ.

However, Christ's resurrected life is not like His life before. Now, things like sin, death, pain, and sadness are all gone. He is a new person who has gone beyond death. Much of what we see in Christ's life is going through and reliving the life Adam was meant to live. This is why Paul describes Christ as being like Adam in 1 Corinthians 15 and Romans 5. But where Adam brought death, Jesus brings life. Jesus doesn't succumb to Satan's temptation, as Adam did. Jesus gives His life in service to His Father and to others, unlike Adam. In a sense, Jesus relives the world in the first days of creation, the world that was perfect until Adam and Eve gave in to sin.

On Good Friday, the sixth day of Holy Week, Jesus relives the creation of man and the fall into sin as He takes on the sins of the world and brings them to their natural conclusions: death. Jesus rests in the tomb on the seventh day of Holy Week, knowing His work is complete, just as His Father's work was completed on the sixth day and He rested on the seventh. When Jesus rises from the dead, He does so in a world that now has someone who lives beyond death. Jesus inaugurates the new creation with His own resurrection. The Early Church did not see the Sunday of Christ's resurrection as the first day of the week because the seven days of creation represent the old world that had fallen into sin. So Christ rises—not on the first day but on the eighth. This is the first day in a new creation that no longer follows the rules of the old one because here death is no longer a possibility.

Being baptized into Christ means following Him through death into new life. It means the new creation isn't simply something we wait for; it already exists in the life of Christ. Eternal life doesn't start when you die. You are already living it. God has promised you that life and has bound you to it through the covenant of Holy Baptism, which brings you into the life of His Son. Your resurrection is assured. It just hasn't happened yet. Baptism is the assurance of your resurrection. Luther says,

> Wherefore St. Paul, in Romans 6[:4], says, "We were buried with Christ by baptism into death." The sooner a person dies after baptism, the sooner is his baptism completed."[16]

Baptism means death, but it is a death that brings you into something truly new. It brings you into a world where death no longer has any power. It is for this reason many baptismal fonts are octagonal. They show that you have entered into the new creation brought about by the new life of Christ. Each side represents a day of creation, with the eighth side reminding us of our connection to the new creation through Baptism. As we are joined to Christ's life in Baptism, we follow Him into that new world as well.

Further in Depth

One of the themes that crops up in Paul's letters is that of adoption. One such instance is found in Romans 8:14–17: "For all who are led by the Spirit of God are sons of God. For you did not receive the spirit of slavery to fall back into fear, but you have received the Spirit of adoption as sons, by whom we cry, 'Abba! Father!' The Spirit Himself bears witness with our spirit that we are children of God, and if children, then heirs—heirs of God and fellow heirs with Christ, provided we suffer with Him in order that we may also be glorified with Him."

The primary issue Paul is dealing with is explaining how those who

16 Luther, *Luther's Works*, vol. 35, 31.

are not descendants of Abraham can presume to call on God. In this particular passage in Romans, Paul makes an important point: if you have received the Spirit, then you are a child of God. It has nothing to do with whether you can claim Abraham as your ancestor and everything to do with whether the Spirit has come to you. Since the Spirit is a major player in the work of Baptism, anytime someone is talking about receiving this Spirit, it should make us think of Baptism.

Galatians 3:18 says, "For if the inheritance comes by the law, it no longer comes by promise; but God gave it to Abraham by a promise." In his commentary on that passage, Luther writes,

> This is undeniable, that before there was a Law, God by a promise granted Abraham the blessing or inheritance, that is, the forgiveness of sins, righteousness, salvation, and eternal life, which means that we are the sons and heirs of God and fellow heirs with Christ (Rom. 8:17). For Genesis clearly says (22:18): "In your Offspring shall all the nations be blessed." There the blessing is granted without regard for the Law or works. For before Moses was born or anyone had thought about the Law, God had already taken the initiative and granted the inheritance.[17]

Luther answers the question, "What is the relationship between God and his people?" His answer, expanding on Paul, is that the promise made to Abraham was always intended for everyone. The promise made to Abraham and expressed in the body through circumcision was a promise given to everyone. All nations will be bound together through Abraham's Offspring, Christ Jesus.

Baptism then answers the question, "How do we become joined to that promise?" The promise hasn't really changed. God still brings us into His

17 Luther, *Luther's Works*, vol. 26 (St. Louis: Concordia Publishing House, 1963), 304.

family by means of His promise. In the Old Testament, that promise was bound to circumcision. In the New Testament, that promise is bound instead to Baptism. We receive the Spirit in Baptism, so everything that is associated with the Spirit becomes true for us as well. We are given the ability to call God "Father" because we are adopted through the Spirit in Baptism. We are children of God because He has claimed us as His own. Christ's own words in Matthew 28:19 that "all nations" should be baptized makes clear that this promise is not just for the Jews but for all people. None are excluded, regardless of their lineage.

I found this theology expressed strongly at the baptismal font in St. James Cathedral in Seattle, Washington. In a large marble square outside the font are etched the words of 1 Peter 2:9: "But you are a chosen race, a royal priesthood, a holy nation, God's own people, that you may declare the wonderful deeds of God who called you out of darkness into marvelous light" (adapted from RSV). Though Peter echoes the words spoken by God to the Israelites, he is now explicitly applying them to the whole Church.

Rather than putting the emphasis on us and our public declaration of faith, as some church bodies will do, Peter is making it entirely about what God does for us. He has claimed us and made us His own. He has made the public declaration that we are His children. We now bear His mark on our foreheads and are His representatives, for we carry the family name Christian, which means "little Christ." Luther expounds on this a bit in his lectures on Titus:

> In Exodus (Ex. 19:5): "You shall be peculiar to Me, a peculiar people." We say, "My own," and Peter says (1 Peter 2:9) "a people for His possession." Vergil speaks of the *peculium*. That is, this is a people which is the property of Christ, in whose midst He dwells, which is devoted to Him, which He looks after as

> He would a flock, to which He has given life. Not only has He rescued it, but He purifies it every day if there is any filth left.[18]

The wording is a bit different, but the sense is the same. We are not just claimed as His children to be sent off on our own. God takes responsibility for us, cares for us, provides for us, and protects us. He puts His name on us and wants each of us individually and the world as a whole to know that we are His people.

Lutheran theologian Edmund Schlink has a brief thought as well:

> "All who are led by the Spirit of God are sons of God" (Rom. 8:14). Indeed, Christ is the eternal Son of God made man, and the Holy Spirit makes us His brothers who die and live with Him and in Him. He makes the believers adopted sons in Him, the incarnate Son. Not only are we "called" children of God, but we "are" so; not only shall we become God's children in the future, but we are that already (1 John 3:1).[19]

We don't need to wait until someday in the distant future, perhaps even waiting until we die, to be worthy of being children of God. Through Baptism, God makes us worthy now. Whatever we might think of ourselves before Baptism, from that point forward we can be confident of our status as members of God's household. Where before we were strangers, now we are His own adopted children.

Hymn Connection

"Baptized into Your Name Most Holy"

Text by Johann Jacob Rambach

This hymn expresses much of what Paul is saying in Romans 6. It uses

18 Luther, *Luther's Works*, vol. 29 (St. Louis: Concordia Publishing House, 1968), 67.

19 Edmund Schlink, *The Doctrine of Baptism*, trans. Herbert J. A. Bouman (St. Louis: Concordia Publishing House, 1972), 62.

Paul's own language and connects it to what takes place in Baptism on more levels. When thinking about weakness and lowliness in regard to the Sacraments, we are usually thinking in terms of sin and how we do not deserve what we are given. This is true, but it becomes an even more powerful message when applied to children, especially infants.

Genesis 17:1–14 explains how eight-day-old infants were circumcised and made a part of the covenant promise of God to His people. Not only are these infants sinners and unworthy of any of God's gifts, but they are physically powerless as well. A child that old has no power to earn Baptism or circumcision or even request it. This makes what they receive a gift in the purest sense of the word.

It also expresses some of what 1 Peter 2 declares as we receive His name and become His people. It is through this covenant promise that a Christian, whether child or adult, has God's name placed on him or her and can formally be considered a child of God. The hymn gives thanks for what God has done through Baptism. But it is also a prayer. It is a prayer that asks God to continue loving you as His own child and to help you learn and grow. It asks Him to help you stay true to the faith you have confessed through eternity.

Questions for Review

6. Have you ever thought about your Baptism as a part of what makes you who you are?

7. How much does your Baptism affect your identity?

God makes a definitive claim on you in your Baptism. You never have to worry or wonder where you belong from that point forward. You are God's child. You are a part of His family and are always welcome in His house. The whole rest of the world could abandon you, but God would still welcome you in with open arms. God stands by His promises and never fails to keep them. If He did fail to keep His promises, He wouldn't be a God worth worshiping.

This is what it means to be a child of God. He isn't a foster parent who is only signing up for a short time. He is adopting you and taking you as His own from this point forward. This relationship doesn't even stop at death. He signs up to be your Father forever and rejoices to share His home with you for eternity.

UNIT 6

Israelites in the Wilderness

Aside from the flood, the other Old Testament event most often reflected on as a basis for Baptism is the crossing of the Red Sea. Luther includes it in his Flood Prayer as well, saying,

> Almighty and eternal God, according to Your strict judgment You condemned the unbelieving world through the flood, yet according to Your great mercy You preserved believing Noah and his family, eight souls in all. You drowned hard-hearted Pharaoh and all his host in the Red Sea, yet led Your people Israel through the water on dry ground, foreshadowing this washing of Your Holy Baptism.[20]

In order to better understand the Red Sea, we should back up a bit and look at what led to the Israelites being at the Red Sea.

- Read Exodus 12:1–28.

1. What is the purpose of the blood on the doorposts?

20 *LSB*, p. 268

2. **How does this use of blood relate to the rainbow after the flood?**

3. **Why does God want them to continue celebrating the Passover in the future?**

There's much in the Passover that relates to Communion, but for now, we're just interested in those things that tell us about Baptism. In this case, the blood on the doorposts functions in a very similar way to the rainbow after the flood. Here again, the blood is not meant for the people but for God. Judgment falls on the land of Egypt, but God sees the lamb's blood on the doorposts and remembers that judgment will pass by that house. The rainbow and the blood both remind God that any punitive judgment that needs to be given in this world is not going to fall on the people under the sign of the covenant.

The Passover event, like circumcision before it, continues to solidify the Israelites' place as God's people. They are the ones who were spared from God's judgment. God will repeatedly look back on the Passover-crossing event as the point that established them as His people. For example, in Exodus 20, God prefaces the Ten Commandments with the reason He has the authority to give them these commandments:

> I am the Lord your God, who brought you out of the land of Egypt, out of the house of slavery. (Exodus 20:2)

They are told to remember how this came to happen. Not that they repeat the same event over and over, for they are not in Egypt anymore, but that they remember how they escaped from Egypt to begin with. In this way, the Passover is already working like Baptism will later work for us in saving us from judgment and the death that goes with it, as well as giving us another way to be known as God's people. Let's take a look at what happens after the Commandments are given.

- Read Exodus 14:1–30.

4. What do Pharaoh and his armies represent here?

5. Who receives this "baptism"?

Like the flood, everyone who enters the Red Sea is "baptized" here. The difference is that Israelites come through unscathed, while Pharaoh and his armies perish in the waters. For those who trust in God, the waters provide salvation. Everyone else finds only destruction here.

Pharaoh embodies unbelief and the power of death. He seeks to enslave the Israelites, crush them down, and destroy them. God shares with His people what Baptism is meant to do. By trusting in Him, we receive life instead of death and freedom from our sinful slavery to unbelief. What's also worth noting is that between the Passover and the crossing, God makes one very important point: "And when the LORD brings you into the land of the Canaanites, the Hittites, the Amorites, the Hivites, and the Jebusites, which He swore to your fathers to give you, a land flowing with milk and honey, you shall keep this service in this month" (Exodus 13:5). God doesn't just tell them that they are leaving but that they have a destination.

There's a goal in mind from the very beginning: the Promised Land. From this point forward, God will lead them, and they will follow. In this sense, the Israelites have "died" to sin and unbelief and are living a new life as the people of God. We remember Paul commenting on this whole idea in Romans 6:6–7: "We know that our old self was crucified with Him in order that the body of sin might be brought to nothing, so that we would no longer be enslaved to sin. For one who has died has been set free from sin." While the crossing is significant on its own, it also leads us to consider the related event of the crossing of the Jordan.

- Read Joshua 3:1–17.

6. In what ways are the crossing of the Jordan and the crossing of the Red Sea similar?

7. How does this event relate to the crossing of the Red Sea?

Here, the Israelites cross a body of water on dry ground by the power and grace of God. In this case, they are not being chased by Pharaoh or anyone else. There is no threat of death. Nevertheless, this is not something they could have achieved on their own, and God has them go through this similar event to illustrate that the two events are related. All of the Laws of Moses were given to the Israelites while they were in the wilderness. The laws were given to help the Israelites learn what it means to live as the people of God and to give them a way to show, by word and deed, that they are not like any other group of people in the world. They are a holy people who have a special relationship with God. Their time in the wilderness is when they start to put this into action and begin living as God's people. It takes some time for them to learn how to do so, but they eventually get there.

All this time in the wilderness tells us something about our own lives as baptized children of God. We are made holy and are told through God's Word what it means to be His people. We learn to live as the people He has made us. We also have received our own promise and are looking forward to it. There is a new promised land, the kingdom of God, which comes into the world wherever Christ is. Thus, we look forward to His return. Baptism is what assures us we will be among the people who will be in that kingdom when it comes.

Israel's wandering in the wilderness for forty years recalls the forty days of rain during the flood of Noah's day. The wandering works similarly to the flood. It is an extended and thorough period of purification that washes people and creation alike to restore them and bring them back to what they were meant to be.

The forty-year journey was never the plan to begin with. God led the Israelites to the Promised Land rather directly from Mount Sinai. However, as they heard the reports from the spies they had sent into the Promised Land, they mistrusted God's abilities and gave in to fear. They ultimately refused the gift God was offering. All of this stemmed from sin. This sin necessitated the same kind of cleansing as the world did in Noah's day, so God leads them on a trek that purges that sinful mistrust from His people and binds them to Him. By keeping them in the wilderness for forty years, God is bodily removing the unbelief from the larger body of people. Obviously, the faithful who do pass into the Promised Land are still sinful, so this is not a complete purging of all sin. Still, it gives us an idea of how severely God deals with sin and how sin becomes a barrier between us and the promised land of the new creation we are looking for in our future.

This makes the two crossings and everything in between one long baptismal event. The people escape from death and unbelief in the Red Sea and are brought into the Promised Land through the Jordan. All the while, they learn to live as God's holy people and are distinct from the world. This tells us a great deal about what God has in store for us when we approach the baptismal font. He is saving us from a great many things, but He is also telling us what awaits us as we follow Him on the way to the promised land in God's new creation.

As I said in Unit 2, our Baptisms are only fulfilled in death. There, everything that God sees in us becomes reality. We look forward to our own promised land and await the day when our baptismal journey will be complete as we cross over to be in God's presence. In that sense, we are joined to the whole host of Israelites as they wander the Sinai Peninsula, following wherever God leads. During our journey, we will also learn to live as God's holy people, people who are distinct from the world around us. One day, as we follow Christ through our own grave and beyond, everything that God had begun in us here will be complete.

Further in Depth

I want to circle back around to the connection between the blood on the doorposts at Passover and the rainbow after the flood. In Galatians 3:23–29, Paul says,

> Now before faith came, we were held captive under the law, imprisoned until the coming faith would be revealed. So then, the law was our guardian until Christ came, in order that we might be justified by faith. But now that faith has come, we are no longer under a guardian, for in Christ Jesus you are all sons of God, through faith. For as many of you as were baptized into Christ have put on Christ. There is neither Jew nor Greek, there

> is neither slave nor free, there is no male and female, for you are all one in Christ Jesus. And if you are Christ's, then you are Abraham's offspring, heirs according to promise.

With that in mind, let's take the connection one step further. We recognize that the Law Paul is specifically referring to earlier in the chapter is the body of Law given to the Israelites through Moses. Paul is telling the Galatian Church about how God's promises work. The Israelites were not God's people because they kept the Law. The Law's main purpose, at least in Paul's current argument, is to point out how far we fall short of keeping it. Since we cannot keep the Law, it holds us captive.

In Galatians 3, Paul explains what makes someone a child of God. God promised Abraham he would have many descendants. One of those descendants would be the promised Savior, Jesus. Abraham wasn't told when all this would happen, just that it truly would happen. Abraham believed God, even though there was no evidence. This trust in God's promise is what makes you a recipient of that promise. The Law given through Moses to the Israelites much later did not make them children of God, for God had already established that through His promise.

We who trust in the promise of our Savior—not that He will come, but that He already has come and has given His life on our behalf—become heirs according to that promise. We become children of God just like Abraham and his descendants. Because we trust in God to provide a Savior, we are saved. In one sense, it is just as easy as that. We are given Christ's righteousness because we trust in Him to save us, and that's all there is to it. While we are saved through Christ, the wording Paul uses here suggests something more.

In Unit 4, we looked into the whole concept of the image of God. We talked about the roles we are given because we are made in the image of God and how the image of God isn't a physical resemblance but a spiritual one. Nevertheless, the wording is important. If I were perfectly righteous, then I would perfectly reflect all of God's love back to Him. Like a mirror, God would look at us and "see" the love He gave us coming back to Him. Since we are all sinners, we are all broken mirrors and do not reflect anything at all. We want to keep it all to ourselves.

This is where Paul's statement becomes important. In Baptism, we "put on Christ" (v. 27). While we are broken mirrors, incapable of reflecting anything, Christ has no such trouble. Christ is God, so by definition, He must be in the image of God. As one might put on a costume, we have put on Christ. So when the Father looks down at us, He doesn't see us at all. He sees only Jesus, and the love He has for us is perfectly reflected back to Him because Christ loves His Father—and all of us—perfectly. Thus, we are restored to the image of God, not because we have done anything special but because Christ is doing the job for us.

I bring all this up here because this passage also brings the rainbow and the blood together in the work of Christ. In my Baptism, I have put on Christ. That means all the promises made to me through Baptism are mine as well. God made a promise to Noah and all creation, and He made a sign of that promise in the rainbow. God made a promise to the Israelites, and He instructed them to make a sign of that promise in the blood of the lamb on the doorposts. When God looks at me and thinks about wiping creation out with a flood, He has to look at it through the rainbow, remembering the promise He made. When He threatened the nation of Egypt with the deaths of their firstborn males, He had to look at the Israelites through the blood of the lamb, remembering His promise. When He looks at me and thinks about bringing judgment against my sin, He has to look at me through Christ, remembering His promise.

Luther reflects on this a bit in his sermon on Romans 13 as he references this passage from Galatians 3:

> [Jesus] is our example and pattern, so that we follow Him and become like Him, clothed in the same virtues He is. About that St. Paul says that we are to put on Christ. Likewise, he writes: "Just as we have borne the image of the man of dust, let us also bear the image of the man of heaven" (1 Corinthians 15 [:49]); and "Put off your old man, which belongs to your former manner of life and is corrupt through deceitful desires, and be renewed in the spirit of your minds and put on the new man, created after the likeness of God in true righteousness and holiness" (Ephesians 4 [:22–24]).[21]

We exchange our dirty, sin-stained clothes for Christ's own robe of righteousness. Christ covers me completely.

The Father already inflicted the punishment for my sin on His Son. Now Christ is glorified and beyond death. Now He lives eternally. I am baptized, so I hide behind Christ. I don't want to come out of hiding, for that would mean I stand on my own, without protection. I would suffer the same sort of fate as an Israelite who stepped outside during the final plague, no longer under the protection of the blood. Judgment would swiftly follow. "Putting on Christ" is one way to see how the promise becomes mine.

Hymn Connection

"Guide Me, O Thou Great Redeemer"

Text by William Williams

This hymn draws on the experience of the Israelites as they travel out of Egypt and make their way toward the land God had promised them. It was God who led them out of Egypt. God kept them safe on their journey. It was God who provided for them along the way. It was God who finally brought them to the Jordan and into the Promised Land.

21 Luther, "Epistle for the First Sunday in Advent," in *Luther's Works*, vol. 75 (St. Louis: Concordia Publishing House, 2013), 23.

The hymn expresses the sentiment of the Israelites, who put their trust in God to save them from beginning to end, acknowledging that God alone could make all this happen. It also makes the important point that should not be overlooked. In our role as priests, one of our responsibilities is to lift up praises to God, both our own and those of creation around us. We are people who have heard God's promises and trusted in Him. More than that, we have seen Him fulfill His promises. Praise is the proper and natural response we offer to God, thanking Him for all He has done for us.

Questions for Review

Consider what it means to "put on Christ." Think about what it means for Him to be living your life just as you live His. If Christ is living your life right alongside you, what does that say about God's willingness to help you through tough times? When you run into some difficulty this week, think about where Jesus is in all of it. What does His presence say about what's going on in your life?

From the time you are baptized, Christ's life and yours are bound together. He lives your life and dies your death perfectly. Unless you reject the grace given to you in Baptism, every moment of every day is one in which God sees His Son's righteousness covering you. The kind of love the Father has for His Son is given to you as well. If the Father gives life again to His Son, then He will do the same for you. In John 17:22–24, Jesus prays,

> The glory that You have given Me I have given to them, that they may be one even as We are one, I in them and You in Me, that they may become perfectly one, so that the world may know that You sent Me and loved them even as You loved Me. Father, I desire that they also, whom You have given Me, may be with Me where I am, to see My glory that You have given Me because You loved Me before the foundation of the world.

If the Father listens to the prayers of His Son, cares for Him, and glorifies Him, He will do the same for you. Prior to this, in John 16, Jesus tells His disciples, "Truly, truly, I say to you, whatever you ask of the Father in My name, He will give it to you. Until now you have asked nothing in My name. Ask, and you will receive, that your joy may be full" (vv. 23–24). The Father won't do anything to you or give you anything that would ultimately harm you. So He won't feed any sinful or selfish desires you might have. However, anything else you ask for, He promises to hear and bless.

UNIT 7

The Baptism of Jesus

The Baptism of Jesus is where all the elements we've examined so far start to come together. Each Gospel book mentions Jesus' Baptism, but none of them gives more than the essentials. Let's take a look.

- Read Matthew 3:13–17.

1. **Who is involved in this scene?**

2. **Why is it important for each of those individuals to be present?**

3. **Why does Jesus need to be baptized?**

4. How does this "fulfill all righteousness" (v. 15)?

Taken all by itself, there just isn't a whole lot to go on here. Without looking at what has come before this point, we wouldn't have any idea why Jesus bothers to do any of this. John the Baptist is completely correct here. He is the sinner, not Jesus. A Baptism of repentance, such as John had been giving, or a new Baptism of grace and forgiveness, such as Jesus later commands, have no use for someone who has never sinned. But Jesus is not operating alone here.

This event is one of the few places we clearly see the Father, Son, and Holy Spirit all visible at the same time. Jesus, standing there in the water with the Father and the Holy Spirit around Him, should remind us of the very first time we see all three persons together: at creation. The Trinity does not appear here by happenstance. The triune God is actively demonstrating what Baptism is all about by recalling the very earliest point in history, when Father, Son, and Holy Spirit take an unformed ball of water and begin transforming it into the world we know. Baptism brings us back to creation, re-creating us into the sinless state and the image of God we were created to have.

This recalls Paul's statement in Romans 6:3–4: "Do you not know that all of us who have been baptized into Christ Jesus were baptized into His death? We were buried therefore with Him by baptism into death, in order that, just as Christ was raised from the dead by the glory of the Father, we too might walk in newness of life." We see here that being "baptized into Christ Jesus" means a great deal more than just eternal life. Eternal life itself doesn't come about all by itself. Sin brings death. So sin must be dealt with so death ceases to exist. Thus, Baptism brings us back to creation, the time before sin. But it doesn't just bring us back to creation—it brings us to the new creation. It's not just a time before sin exists but a time when sin can *never* exist. Obviously, sin still exists today, but God no longer sees it and no longer treats us as sinners. He treats us as if the work begun in Baptism had already reached its fulfillment and we have been made completely clean.

Jesus is living the life Adam should have lived. He doesn't need to fulfill His own righteousness. He is fulfilling Adam's, and by extension, the righteousness of every sinner since. We are made righteous in Christ, and our Baptism has power because Christ prepared it for us. In the Large Catechism, Luther says,

> Therefore it is not simply a natural water, but a divine, heavenly, holy, and blessed water—praise it in any other terms you can—all by virtue of the Word, which is a heavenly, holy Word that no one can sufficiently extol, for it contains and conveys all of God. From the Word it derives its nature as a sacrament, as St. Augustine taught, "*Accedat verbum ad elementum et fit sacramentum*." This means that when the Word is added to the element or the natural substance, it becomes a sacrament, that is, a holy, divine thing and sign.[22]

The triune God distills His creative and redemptive work into the water here. Just as God declares the anointing oil holy, to be used in making others holy, now Jesus claims the water as His, for making sinners holy and righteous. It should be noted that *Christ* and *Messiah* mean "Anointed One." All the references we saw earlier to anointing are applied now to Christ. The Church talks about Jesus as being a Prophet, Priest, and King, and here is where all of that happens. Through Him, we, too, become prophets, priests, and kings or queens through our own baptismal anointing.

22 Large Catechism, Part 4, paragraphs 17 and 18.

The Spirit's presence here has a bit more for us to consider. Let's take a look at Jesus' later discussion of Baptism.

- Read John 3:1–8.

5. According to Jesus, what is the role of the Spirit in Baptism?

6. What does Jesus mean when He says, "kingdom of God"?

Here we find a Pharisee named Nicodemus doing what God's people were always meant to do. He goes to Jesus and seeks wisdom and understanding. Jesus' statements are confusing, but Nicodemus sticks with it in an effort to learn more, and he is not disappointed. Jesus spends some time talking about the Holy Spirit and what His role is in Baptism.

We saw the Spirit at Jesus' Baptism, but all we're told in the Gospel accounts is that the Spirit marked Jesus as the Messiah. Here, Jesus tells Nicodemus that the Spirit is integral to this notion of rebirth. In order to be "born again" (or "born from above," depending on how you translate the word), you need the Spirit.

This rebirth idea clearly confuses Nicodemus, but Jesus isn't saying anything new here. Looking at all the events we've examined, Jesus is just explaining again what Baptism does. If I am born with the sin of Adam, which means I do not have the image of God and can't fulfill any of the duties God created me to do, then I need to be born again, just without the sin. So Jesus tells Nicodemus that this is exactly what Baptism does.

The Spirit's role here might be a little puzzling too, but going back to Genesis 2:7 gives us the answer:

> Then the LORD God formed the man of dust from the ground and breathed into his nostrils the breath of life, and the man became a living creature.

The Hebrew word for *breath* is the same word they use for *wind* or *spirit.* So the Father puts His Spirit in Adam, and Adam comes to life. Thus, if I need to be reborn, it must be because I do not have the Spirit in me. Paul tells us this again in Romans 8:10–11:

> But if Christ is in you, although the body is dead because of sin, the Spirit is life because of righteousness. If the Spirit of Him who raised Jesus from the dead dwells in you, He who raised Christ Jesus from the dead will also give life to your mortal bodies through His Spirit who dwells in you.

In Baptism, we receive the Holy Spirit and are reborn. We are brought from death into life by the power of the Spirit.

Jesus makes Baptism a requirement for entering the kingdom of God. Throughout the Gospel books, Jesus constantly teaches about the kingdom of God. One of the biggest points He tries to get across is that His kingdom is not a physical kingdom with physical borders. His kingdom exists wherever the King is reigning. Since the King is Jesus Himself and Jesus is God, that means you need to be fit to be in the King's presence if you are to be in His kingdom. That means being cleansed of your sin. This is one of the major reasons Baptism comes before Communion since that is where you come into the physical presence of the King in the bread and the wine. In the next unit, we'll look at how Baptism comes to be a sacrament to begin with.

Further in Depth

In all this discussion of Jesus' Baptism and what He says about Baptism in John 3, we should take a moment and talk about the work of the Spirit a bit more as well. In both places, we see the Spirit at work in Baptism. Each person of the Trinity is involved in all aspects of salvation, but the Spirit often flies under the radar a bit. That's sort of His job anyway. He brings us to Christ, and all His work is geared toward bringing us in where the triune God is freely offering salvation.

That means the Spirit is very active in Baptism since it is one of the main gifts God gives to His people. We already talked a bit about the Spirit's role in bringing life. We confess in the Nicene Creed that the Spirit is "the Lord and giver of life," and His work in bringing what is inanimate and dead to life in creation and in re-creation is where that comes from.

The Spirit also brings us to faith. Faith trusts in God's promises, so faith is essential to being a disciple. Those promises are found in God's Word, and it is the Spirit who allows us to trust what we find there. Paul says this in 2 Timothy 3:16–17: "All Scripture is breathed out by God and profitable for teaching, for reproof, for correction, and for training in righteousness, that the man of God may be complete, equipped for every good work." I said before that in Hebrew *breath* and *spirit* are the same word. Though Paul writes in Greek, he is a Jewish scholar, and it is not strange at all to connect those two ideas here again.

God's Word carries along His Spirit so that wherever His Word is found, the Spirit comes along with it. That also means when God's Word is encountered either through verbal proclamation or through the written text, the Spirit is active and working in the one who hears or reads it. If the hearer is not yet a Christian, the Spirit is working to help him trust what God says to him in His Word. If the person is a Christian, then the Spirit is reminding her of what God has said and helping her to continue trusting in God and what He has promised.

Baptism builds on the foundation that has already been laid in faith. This makes what the Spirit does in bringing unbelievers to faith and what He does in Baptism related but distinct. We might say that once someone is baptized, the Spirit turns the volume up. God's Word is heard and understood more clearly because He has brought a greater level of restoration into the life of the baptized Christian.

The Spirit is active wherever the Word is proclaimed. The Spirit can engender faith and trust whenever someone hears the promises of God. We've seen how the Spirit does a great many things in and for God's people. How the Spirit works in one place is not necessarily how He works in another. The biblical themes for Baptism do connect with salvation, but they take what is given in faith and add even more richness and depth. It is as if what is given in faith is an outline, and now the Spirit begins filling in that outline with beauty and color. In Baptism, the Spirit gives our faith direction and purpose. Just as we saw in our discussion of anointing and the image of God, we are not simply saved. We are saved in order to do the work of God. The Spirit, who brought us to faith in Christ, now dwells within us to carry out the work we've been given to do.

When we looked at some of the extra elements of the flood narrative in Unit 3, one of the things that came up was a dove. The Spirit's appearance in the form of a dove at Jesus' Baptism is probably one you will recall a little better than the dove Noah sends from the ark. The dove in Noah's day is not something that will necessarily connect to anything in the future, for God does not specifically tell us it will. But, like the numbers that show up in the passage we have already looked at, we should not be surprised to see the Spirit as a dove here.

In Noah's time, the dove comes at the end, as the floodwaters are receding. The judgment against sin has passed. Now creation has been restored to a state near what it was at the beginning. With that in mind, it comes as no surprise the form the Spirit takes here would be a dove. Jesus' Baptism indicates the time for fearing God's judgment against sin has also passed. Jesus' arrival and Baptism tells us He is here to live our lives as we were meant to. Since He is living our lives perfectly, we are safe from God's judgment.

Given that both events are baptismal in nature, the Spirit's form as a dove becomes a natural choice. Anyone seeing Jesus' Baptism who is familiar with the story of Noah should at least be thinking about where else the dove has shown up in Scripture. Since the word shows up nowhere else in Scripture except as poetic or figurative language, it becomes a pretty strong clue that the Spirit is directing people to the one other place a dove makes an appearance in Scripture. It should be obvious to those watching that what happened in Noah's day is somehow happening once again. Once, long ago, a dove indicated salvation was at hand, so a dove is once again telling people salvation has arrived.

We've talked about the number *40* already, but it shows up here again—not in Jesus' Baptism but immediately afterward. Jesus walks out in the wilderness to be alone for forty days. At the end of those forty days, Jesus is tempted by Satan. Though Satan offers Him many things, Jesus does not give in to the temptation.

Since Jesus is reliving our lives, getting right everything we get wrong all the way back to the beginning, we see a reenactment of the Garden of Eden. Satan arrives on the scene and begins twisting God's Word so as to introduce doubt and to offer things God has not offered. Where Adam and Eve gave in, Jesus does not. He makes it through the ordeal somewhat hungrier, but He is otherwise none the worse for wear. Satan tried his best and failed.

That Jesus does not give in here shows that Satan's lies cannot prevail against God. Jesus thwarts the tempter's power. Jesus undoes that first sin by reliving that event and getting it right. He defeats one of His enemies here and restores the original state of creation.

This is similar to how Jesus defeats death. The Early Church theologian Athanasius says, "Now if by the sign of the Cross, and by faith in Christ, death is trampled down, it must be evident before the tribunal of truth that it is none other than Christ Himself that has displayed trophies and triumphs over death, and made him lose all his strength."[23]

The Spirit aids all this work, and Scripture has alluded to this a couple of times. We've seen the dove active as Noah sends it out as the waters recede, but we actually see that Spirit-directed connection a bit earlier in that passage. Genesis 8:1 says, "And God made a wind blow over the earth, and the waters subsided." Where we see the word *wind*, the Hebrew reader again sees the same word as *breath* and *spirit*, or, more properly for us, *Spirit*.

Just like in the earliest moments of creation, where the Spirit hovered over the face of the unformed waters, here again, God sends His Spirit, and the work of creation begins anew as the waters subside. In the midst of the waters that brought death, God sends His life-giving Spirit to restore the world. The work that Christ will later do as He tramples down death is made known by the Spirit, who is a part of the process the whole time.

Lest we think this Old Testament, Spirit, and Baptism theme is just coincidence, God gives us another example. In Exodus 14, as the Israelites are huddled at the edge of the Red Sea, watching Pharaoh's chariots rushing toward them, God sends yet another wind to part the waters. Yet again God breathes/*Spirits* into the waters and provides life and salvation in the midst of death.

23 Athanasius of Alexandria, "On the Incarnation of the Word," in *A Select Library of Nicene and Post-Nicene Fathers of the Christian Church*, Series 2, vol. 4 (Grand Rapids, MI: Eerdmans, 1957), 51.

Taken together with the dove imagery, God is weaving the flood and the crossing of the Red Sea together with Jesus' Baptism and showing us how many of the elements we have come to understand in Baptism have been there for a very long time. Baptism is not an afterthought of God or some sort of plan B. Baptism has been the goal all along, and the Spirit has been a part of it the entire time.

Hymn Connection

"To Jordan Came the Christ, Our Lord"

Text by Martin Luther

This hymn of Luther's may not be as well known as others, but it comes with some distinctive Luther trademarks. Luther often has a hard time getting everything he wants to say in just a couple of stanzas, so his hymns tend to be pretty lengthy. The seven stanzas of this hymn unpack the physical and spiritual aspects of Jesus' Baptism in the Jordan.

Luther first explains that Jesus came to the Jordan to be baptized by John. That might be an obvious comment, but the historical element is one of the aspects of Christianity that sets it apart from other religions. When we talk about Jesus being baptized and what that does for us, we aren't just talking metaphorically. Jesus truly did get baptized. This event stands in history as a true event to, as Jesus says, "fulfill all righteousness" (Matthew 3:15). Without the historical events, such as the flood or the crossing of the Red Sea, the promises God makes would have nothing to anchor to. We would have no proof that God does indeed fulfill His promises, and we would have no basis to trust Him for anything.

But those events did happen. Thus, all the themes we have explored, some of which Luther relays here as well, are all sure and certain. Baptism is a cleansing from transgression, an entry into new life, a joining of God's family, and more, all because God has established those themes and ideas and brought them together here with Jesus in the Jordan.

Questions for Review

7. **In what ways does the Spirit work through God's Word to guide you during the week?**

8. **How does the repentance and new obedience the Spirit works in you through Law and Gospel show He is active in your daily life?**

9. **What does His Word direct you to do?**

The Spirit is a part of Christian life every moment of every day. The Spirit is active in God's Word. So wherever God's Word is read and proclaimed, the Spirit is there. However, the Spirit is active in a more personal way when it comes to Baptism. As Jesus explains in John 3, those who are baptized are born again of water and the Spirit. The Spirit is within you, bringing you new life.

It is the Spirit who enables you to live once again in the image of God because it is the Spirit who brings you into Christ's life. The Spirit is always leading you to Christ. That means everything you do as a prophet, priest, or king or queen is directed by Him. That covers quite a lot of things. Some of those things are easily defined, like when you pray for someone or something, when you talk about God, when you care for someone else, or anything else like that. However, the Spirit is also simply helping you live more like Christ. Every temptation you avoid, every humble request for forgiveness, and every moment you find yourself trusting God is driven by the Spirit as well.

So aside from the tangible proof Baptism provides that the Spirit is with you, the Spirit continues to show Himself to you throughout your life. Any time you find yourself doing any of those things, the Spirit is there working in and through you. Paul says, "Therefore I want you to understand that no one speaking in the Spirit of God ever says, 'Jesus is accursed!' and no one can say 'Jesus is Lord' except in the Holy Spirit" (1 Corinthians 12:3). If you still trust in God's promises to save and give life, the Spirit is still with you. He works continually to keep you in the faith and to help you better live out your Christian life and calling every day.

UNIT 8

Discipleship

It's great that God gives us so much information about what Baptism does, but until He actually tells us to do it, there's nothing tying His grace to the waters of Baptism. So let's take a look at what Jesus says about it.

- Read Matthew 28:16–20.

1. **What are the two components of becoming a disciple?**

2. **What does Baptism consist of?**

3. **Why does discipleship only require these two things?**

Teaching and Baptism are the dual requirements for discipleship. Jesus makes it surprisingly easy to hit the mark. Yet both requirements carry a great deal of weight. Through teaching and Baptism, Jesus calls each of us to do essentially what the Twelve did. They were taught by God Himself. They followed Him through His life and learned to put into practice the things He said and did. They learned to be like Him. But in order to carry out the things Jesus was saying and doing, they needed to be given the ability to do so.

Baptism has a great deal to do with justification—making us right in the eyes of God. It takes our faith and gives it a new focus and direction. Now we see Baptism also has a great deal to do with sanctification. It helps us to live the life God has always intended for us to live. With the Holy Spirit and the life of Christ within us, we are made to be like the people we were created to be.

Baptism itself is also quite simple. You have to draw a bit on the historical understanding of Baptism as a ritual washing, but Jesus changes it slightly by making it a washing specifically in the triune name of God. This, and only this, is the Sacrament of Baptism. Without a washing in the triune name of God, you have no Baptism. This is what God has promised will carry His grace and what will work the wonders He has prepared the world for.

With that in mind and as disciples of Christ ourselves, it's time to tackle some of the bigger questions.

4. Knowing what you know now, should the Church baptize infants?

Jesus doesn't specify whether you teach people about the faith and then baptize them (as usually happens with adults) or baptize them and then teach them about the faith they've been baptized into (as usually happens with infants). He only states that both need to happen for someone to be a disciple. So here Jesus doesn't differentiate between children and adults. All are commanded to be disciples through baptizing and teaching.

That alone is enough reason to baptize infants, but our study of Old Testament events gives us quite a bit more. Looking at how circumcision relates to Baptism, we see that God does not request but commands that eight-day-old boys be circumcised. As sinners, we do not naturally seek out God's gifts. We must be brought to a place where we can be put in contact with those gifts. Those boys are born bearing the curse of Adam, and through circumcision, that curse begins to be undone as they are formally made God's people.

The nature of that sin hasn't changed since the days of Abraham. We still bear the curse of Adam from the moment of our conception. We are not born as one of God's people. We must be made into one. God saw the need for this in Old Testament days, and that need is still there. Children need that promise as much as everyone else.

Since children are sinners, that also means everything related to the image of God and God's promises of salvation are there for them as well. Children still need the promise made through the rainbow and the blood of the Passover lamb that saves them from judgment and death. Children need the baptismal anointing so they can be prophets, priests, and kings or queens, just as God intended. Thus, children have just as much reason to be baptized as adults do. Children, too, are subject to death. They need to be joined to Christ's death and resurrection. That way, as they grow older and learn the significance of their Baptism, they will have that same concrete assurance of eternal life that God gives to all who come to the font.

5. How can we remember our Baptism after it has happened?

This is a question that doesn't have just one right answer. The Church has used many tools to help us remember how God is at work in our lives through our Baptism and to keep that work in mind even after we've been baptized. One tool is the sign of the cross. The sign of the cross is usually made on the ones who are being baptized to show that they are receiving the death and resurrection of Christ through their Baptism. That never ceases to be true. There are many places in the worship service that recall our Baptism, such as the Invocation, where we remember that it is the triune God who has invited us into His house, and it is He who put His name on us in Baptism.

The first half of the worship service, the Service of the Word, is built for disciples as well. This part of the service emphasizes God's Word and our response to it. This is the primary joy of disciples, and we are disciples through our Baptism. The worship service is designed to help us grow as disciples as we continue to learn from God.

The liturgical year is the Church's way of walking through the life of Christ. Just as the Twelve did in Jesus' day, we continue to walk through the life of Christ today. Listening to the words of our Lord and watching Him work is how we learn to speak and act as He did. All this draws on our role as disciples.

These are just a few places where our Baptism continues to flow through our lives in the world today, but there are many more. A thorough study of how God has prepared the world for Baptism will help us see how He continues to work in us and through us to make us His people. Baptism is truly a great and wonderful gift, such that God has spent a long time through the Old Testament developing the rich theology of the Sacrament for us to appreciate and use today.

6. Given what we've studied, are there reasons rebaptism might be acceptable?

The themes we've looked at state pretty conclusively that baptizing someone a second (or third, fourth, or even more) time simply doesn't make any sense. Circumcision, for instance, isn't something that is intended to be repeated (if that were even possible). Once you are a child of the promise, you remain a child of the promise, with all the attendant benefits and responsibilities. You may abdicate this role, but that doesn't change what God has offered to you.

The events of the flood or at the Red Sea are also not things to be repeated. In fact, in Deuteronomy 17, God forbids the people from returning to Egypt since that would mean a return to the sin and slavery He had saved them from. All these events worked to establish the people involved as recipients of His promises. God's promises never become invalid, and He never rescinds them. Thus, rebaptizing doesn't fit with any of the themes we've discussed. Rather, it runs very contrary to what those themes have communicated to us.

There are denominations that support or require this sort of practice. In some cases, this is because they only see Baptisms done in their churches as valid. The Lutheran Church does not hold this particular view. Jesus' command in Matthew 28:19 is that the Baptism be done "in the name of the Father and of the Son and of the Holy Spirit." Where water and the name of the triune God are present, there is a valid Baptism. Whenever a person has received a Baptism with water and the triune name, he has received a valid Baptism regardless of who did it. Since Catholics, Eastern Orthodox, and certain other denominations will conduct Baptisms this way, we have no problem with them and accept them just as we would a Baptism done in a Lutheran church.

Other denominations will see Baptism as a way of calling the Spirit to strengthen their faith and encourage them in their Christian living. While the Spirit is most certainly active in Baptism, this view implies that the Spirit left, stopped working, or is waiting for the Christian to recommit before He continues.

The Nicene Creed affirms "one Baptism for the remission of sins." The Nicene Creed is one of the earliest and most universal confessions of faith in the Christian Church. It states that there is one kind of Baptism that offers this (a water Baptism done in the name of the triune God) and that this Baptism is only meant to be done once. The Creed was accepted by the Early Church because it clearly states what Scripture reveals. These ideas that Baptism can or should be done more than once only became widespread with reformers outside of Lutheran circles and were never a part of the Church prior to that.

7. What sort of baptismal imagery can you find around your church? What sorts of themes do you see on display? Do these themes connect with other theological themes you see around your church?

I mentioned earlier that many baptismal fonts are octagonal, alluding to the concept of the eighth day. Many fonts also have other images engraved, such as a shell or a dove. More elaborate ones may have Bible verses or a picture of Christ at His Baptism. The placement of the font and other images can also say something all on its own. Some churches will put their baptismal fonts right in front of the chancel so that the font is always in view. This suggests Baptism should be a constant reminder of what God has done and is doing in our lives. Other churches will put the font right inside the sanctuary or even just outside the entrance in the narthex. This reinforces the idea of Baptism as our entrance into God's kingdom and where we are adopted as His children.

Neither of these ideas is better than the other, but they do bring out different ways of looking at Baptism. There isn't a "right" place to put a baptismal font since the Bible doesn't speak to this. However, Baptism is meant to be a constant reminder of the grace God has given us.

You may also have pictures around your church referencing Baptism in one way or another. Some churches also commemorate Baptisms that have been done there on a banner or a bulletin board. It's not unusual to see a picture of Jesus' Baptism depicted in churches. Sometimes pictures of the Passover or the flood also make an appearance, but these are more rare. With the importance of the sacraments, we should always be challenging ourselves to find ways of making the sacraments and the theology that goes with them more prominent.

8. Looking ahead, what could your church do to help members remember Baptism and think about what it does?

9. What are things you can do to help you remember the gifts given to you in Baptism when you're outside church?

FURTHER IN DEPTH

Baptism is an important, even essential, part of Christian life. As such, it has a particular place and function in our lives. As in the case of issues like infant Baptism, if we misunderstand or misuse Baptism, it won't be able to carry out the full extent of what it tries to accomplish. The same is true of rebaptism. Practices like this end up muddying the waters, as it were, and confuse Christians about the purpose and scope of Baptism. This is why it is imperative that we take the time to study the sacraments in depth and learn how they provide the foundation for the whole life of God's Church.

The first part of the process for all Christians is the Holy Spirit creating faith in Christ our Savior through the Word and Sacraments. Paul says simply, "So faith comes from hearing, and hearing through the word of Christ" (Romans 10:17). Wherever God's Word is encountered, either through a church service, a quiet discussion between friends, or a Bible found in the drawer of a hotel nightstand, the Spirit promises to be active and at work, offering God's promises of forgiveness, life, and salvation. The Spirit works in the heart of the hearer to trust those promises. This trust is the essence of faith. The believer trusts that God can and will make good on what He promises.

Now that we've explored Baptism in depth, you can see that Baptism takes those promises and amplifies them. God gives concrete examples of forgiveness, of life, and of salvation. He shows us what that salvation looks like and, more important, what it means for us both now and in eternity. But like everything else God offers, it is a gift, a promise. Like someone offering me a Christmas present, I can accept what is given or I can choose to reject it, but I can't demand someone to give it to me. If I could, it would no longer be a gift.

The driving force behind the Sacraments is the same way God has always interacted with His people: through His Word. God's Word is what makes the Sacraments do what they do. God promises that when His name is used in connection with the water, all those baptismal gifts are a part of the package. In the Large Catechism, Luther says,

> It is often objected, "If Baptism is itself a work and you say that works are of no use for salvation, what becomes of faith?" To this you may answer: Yes, it is true that our works are of no use for salvation. Baptism, however, is not our work, but God's (for, as was said, you must distinguish Christ's Baptism quite clearly from a bath-keeper's baptism). God's works, however, are salutary and necessary for salvation, and they do not exclude but rather demand faith, for without faith they could not be grasped. Just by allowing the water to be poured over you, you do not receive Baptism in such a manner that it does you any good. But it becomes beneficial to you if you accept it as God's command and ordinance, so that, baptized in the name of God, you may receive in the water the promised salvation. This the hand cannot do, nor the body, but the heart must believe it.[24]

Seminarians will sometimes be challenged to explain why the church doesn't go out to ball games and amusement parks with water guns spraying everyone down and baptizing them. Forcing Baptism on someone is to try and force someone to accept a gift. What God offers is truly a gift. He doesn't force anyone to accept it, and neither should we. At the same time, Jesus' command in Matthew 28 also tells us teaching and Baptism go together. Someone who is baptized without any intention of being taught is disrespecting and misusing the gift God has offered. If they have no intention of becoming a disciple, then they are taking God's gift and then throwing it away.

24 Large Catechism, Part 4, paragraphs 35 and 36.

If you continue your study of the sacraments, you'll see that Baptism (and all the theology that comes with it) is a lead-in to Communion. Communion builds on everything Baptism does. Without Baptism, Communion cannot operate in the manner intended. That means Christian life is a progression. God's Word is what powers all of this from beginning to end. Our lives are built around that trust we have in God's promises, both for our lives here in this world and into eternity.

All the baptismal themes we've explored involve salvation in one way or another. They all attest to the magnitude of what God has done for us. From the very beginning, salvation is always connected to faith. This doesn't change with the Sacraments. Salvation is still through faith alone.

The working of faith is one of those things we as Christians desperately try to make sense of, but it is not something within our power to determine or understand. That God holds the knowledge of how faith works is meant to be a comfort. He tells us very plainly how the Holy Spirit creates faith in us when we hear the proclamation of the Gospel—whether it is God's spoken Word or the Word working in and with the water of Baptism—and trust in the promise He makes to us there. Baptism doesn't save us because it is some kind of get-out-of-jail-free card. It saves us because Christ is the one using His Word in the water to build upon and strengthen our trust in God to care for us as His own.

John the Baptist's response to being near Jesus shows us that even an unborn child can trust in his Savior. A mother who goes to church before her child is born has already given her child the chance to hear the Gospel message and bring that child into the presence of his or her Savior. The opportunity has been given to that child to hear and respond just as John the Baptist did and to be saved.

Whether children die before or after Baptism, if they have been in the presence of their Savior and heard His promise to them, then we trust that the Spirit has been at work. We don't know what truly goes on in the hearts of anyone aside from ourselves. We don't truly know whether anyone else has faith or not. It isn't something God has given us to know or judge. What we do know with certainty is what Nehemiah and others throughout Scripture recalled: "But You are a God ready to forgive, gracious and merciful, slow to anger and abounding in steadfast love, and did not forsake them" (Nehemiah 9:17). God can and does have mercy on the weakest and lowliest, and He delights in doing so.

It's true that infants are unlikely to understand much of anything Scripture teaches, but knowledge is not the same as faith. Certainly, knowledge should be there, but that is part of the life of a disciple. Knowledge grows with time spent in God's Word as each of us is able to understand it. A baby simply hasn't had the time and doesn't have the ability to understand all of the theology of salvation. But a baby does know how to trust, which is the essence of faith.

Still, whether you came to faith as a child or as an adult, you probably don't remember the exact moment you came to faith. In this sinful world where doubts constantly assail us, you might start to question your faith. If you can't remember when you came to faith, then maybe that means you never really did.

This is why Baptism takes the form it does, as a single event in the life of each Christian. We don't know much about the faith life of Noah prior to the flood. As a sinful man, it's a certainty that doubts crept in regarding God's promise, whether He would send the flood and whether He would save Noah from it. The flood gave Noah something concrete he would always be able to look back at and remember. Whatever he was before the flood, at the very least from that point forward, he would know he was righteous in the eyes of God. He must be, for he wouldn't have survived otherwise.

Our Baptism does the same for us. Even if you can't remember the exact day and time you first trusted God's promises, Baptism makes that detail unimportant. God has claimed you in Baptism. He won't reject you or revoke His promise to you. That's why whenever Luther questioned his salvation, he would always recall that he had been baptized.

Baptism stands as a clear sign in your past that God has been and continues to be at work. Your Baptism is a reminder to you of what God has done. But it is also a reminder to God of what He has promised you.

As we saw in the first unit, Baptism is very much about forgiveness and salvation, but that doesn't mean it is identical to faith. God differentiates them for a reason. Baptism gives us more of everything God first offered through the hearing of His Word. Everything is bigger and more profound. Faith, Baptism, and Communion must each hold their own place for them to build up Christian life in the manner they are intended. Letting each do the job they were created for allows us to flourish and grow in the progression God has designed.

Hymn Connection

"O Christ, Who Called the Twelve"

Text by Herman G. Stuempfle, Jr.

Though this hymn refers more to the beginning of Jesus' ministry and His calling of the Twelve rather than the end, the purpose of the hymn is to describe the life of a disciple. The job of any disciple of Christ, whether one of the Twelve or any baptized Christian, is to follow in the footsteps of our Lord and Teacher. We go where He goes and do what He does. In so doing, we learn to be more like Him.

The hymn asks Jesus to do for us what He did for the Twelve. It asks Him to teach us as He taught them. It asks Him to help us learn what it means to share His love with those who need it and how to live a life of service to God and to our neighbor. It asks Him to strengthen our faith in times of doubt and strife so that we may stand fast. The Twelve did not figure out what they needed to do right away. They had their entire lives to learn what it meant to be disciples, for discipleship means a lifetime of learning. We ask Jesus to make us His disciples and to teach us our whole lives.

Questions for Review

10. What does the life of a disciple look like during the week?

11. How can you continue learning and growing in your faith outside of church?

The life of a disciple never stops, not even in death. Christ alone leads you from life to death to new life. He continues teaching us because we never stop needing to learn from Him. Church is the most important place because this is where Christ promises to be present with us. The service is the most important time because this is when He promises to be there. Our lives focus on those times we get to spend with Christ in person, but they don't end there. We are still disciples even outside of the church building. That means He continues to present us with ways to learn and grow spiritually.

We find opportunities to share the love of Christ with our neighbor just as Jesus' original twelve disciples did. They were learning to love others by watching their Lord and Teacher at work, and we carry on that same work today. This is also why we spend time in prayer and in the study of Scripture throughout the week. Christ is still speaking to us. Christ is always speaking to us in one way or another, even if it's just to remind us He's with us.

Leader Guide

Note to Leader

The Lutheran Church has always understood Baptism to be one of the greatest gifts God has given His people. As it is one of the few acts Jesus explicitly tied to God's forgiveness and grace, it's little wonder Martin Luther and theologians like him throughout the centuries wrote extensively about Baptism.

Of course, the Bible itself talks about Baptism quite a bit as well. Jesus' famous discussion with Nicodemus in John 3 is all about Baptism and what it does. Jesus directs His disciples to baptize before His ascension. John's Gospel even tells us the disciples were quite active in baptizing during Jesus' ministry. Paul talks about Baptism in some detail in his Epistle to the Romans. Let's also not forget Jesus' forerunner, John, known specifically as "the Baptist," or "the Baptizer."

Though Baptism is described by Jesus and the apostles after Him and has been an integral part of the Church ever since, God had been laying the groundwork for Baptism from the very beginning. All the ideas associated with Baptism have been seen before, just maybe not in the ways you might have thought. God did not simply drop Baptism on the Church and expect His people to figure it out. He used the whole period of the Old Testament to prepare the Church for what Baptism will do. That means if we really want to understand the full extent of what God intended Baptism to do, we need to back up and look through the Old Testament to see what God has put there to teach us about it.

This Bible study is designed to look at many of the events of history and how they relate to our understanding of Baptism. There are a great many events in the Old Testament that tell us something about what God is doing for us in Baptism. In this study, we will cover the following:

The Flood—God saves Noah through a worldwide flood in one of the most momentous events in the Old Testament. In so doing, He sets the stage for much of what we know about Baptism.

Creation—You might not think so at first glance, but everything that happens in the flood is a reflection of what takes place during creation. In order to understand the flood, we have to understand creation.

The Image of God—During creation, God creates man in His image. The phrase "image of God" gets used a lot in theology. It is also crucial to our understanding of Baptism and is the basis for why Jesus is the Christ.

Circumcision—This command of God to Abraham doesn't get quite as much attention as some of the other themes we'll look at, but it is one of the main ways the Israelites come to understand who they are as God's people. Consequently, it has much to say about who we are as God's people today.

Israelites in the Wilderness—The other main theme that establishes the Israelites' identity as God's people involves their time in the wilderness: the Passover, their crossing into the Promised Land, and everything in between.

The Baptism of Jesus—One of the most obvious places to look to understand Baptism is Jesus' own Baptism. However, we cannot fully grasp the importance of what Jesus does here until we have seen everything that came beforehand.

Discipleship—Baptism is truly a sacrament commanded by God. As such, it is important for us to consider what role God wants it to have in His Church. We need to look at what He tells us to do to know what we should do with it today.

This list is by no means exhaustive. Most of these themes overlap one another to some degree, which reinforces the ideas God is trying to communicate through them. Other Bible studies and theological documents that discuss Baptism will often look at overarching themes—such as "new life"—and will put the various Bible passages into the appropriate baptismal theme. The approach we will use here starts with the events themselves and looks at what they are doing on their own before starting to draw parallels. This will prevent us from reading into these events what we already believe about Baptism. Starting with the text allows God to speak for Himself and helps us see how much He has done to prepare the world for the wonders of the Sacrament.

UNIT 1

Introduction

What is Baptism? This may sound like a rather ridiculous question for anyone who has been confirmed in the Lutheran Church. "It's a Means of Grace," you might say. Or perhaps it's "water and the Word." Both are true. If you really remember your Small Catechism, you might even pull out Luther's great statement: "It works forgiveness of sins, rescues from death and the devil, and gives eternal salvation to all who believe this, as the words and promises of God declare" (Baptism, Second Part).

It can't really be much simpler than that, can it? Luther sums it up pretty nicely there. It sounds pretty great. I mean, who wouldn't want all that stuff, especially when all you have to do is get a little wet? Maybe, though, if you spend any time really thinking about it, you might find yourself wondering, "How does Baptism do all this stuff?" You could go back to your Small Catechism again and find that answer that says it's God's Word along with the water that does such great things, but that's not really the question. Obviously, God can do whatever He wants any way He wants to do it. So why Baptism? What makes it so special? Why did He decide to do things this way? We have to be a little careful because God doesn't always reveal the hows and whys of what He does. But if it really is that important, you'd think He'd explain it a bit.

I'll throw you another curve ball to really get things rolling. Are you sure Baptism actually is special? I mean *really* sure? Do you really need

Baptism at all?

Let's keep all this in the back of our minds for a moment and take a look at a couple of Bible passages and discuss them.

- Read 1 John 1:5–10.

1. What does John say God does for those who confess their sins to Him?

DISCUSSION NOTE: Look at what God says about us. What is our status before Him? How does that status change when we confess our sins to Him? Consider that the Greek word used here for confession means "to say the same thing." God has declared us sinners, and by confessing, we agree with Him. But rather than receiving punishment for our acceptance of guilt, we receive God's promised forgiveness.

- Read Psalm 32:1–5.

2. What does King David say was the result of his confession?

DISCUSSION NOTE: Does David suggest God's forgiveness is only given for certain sins or that it is temporary? Is David confident of God's response to his confession? David is truly sorrowful for his sins, but he knows his sin isn't the end of him.

If you're familiar with the historic Lutheran liturgy, you might recognize these passages and their connection to Confession and Absolution. Both passages affirm God's free grace. They both acknowledge how willing God is to forgive. John tells us forgiveness is God's natural response to our confession of sins. In his commentary on 1 John, Dr. Bruce Schuchard says,

> Here, then, in simple terms and without argument John states that, because Jesus is in all things faithful, because he himself is the embodiment of righteousness, we can in all things rely on him. At times, some have surmised that God would

> have to forget the righteous demands of the Law in order to forgive, like some feeble old man who, both consciously and unconsciously, overlooks many of the faults of those he loves. And yet nothing could be further from the truth. Jesus forgives precisely because he can be counted upon in every way to keep his word and at the same time to accomplish and to be what is right. Indifference toward sin is no act of faithfulness; forgiving sin is, on account of the Son's own willing sacrifice of his blood for those he loves.[1]

King David also remarks that God heard his confession, God forgave that sin, and David counts it a great blessing. Luther says of Psalm 32:5,

> This is in contrast to those in whom deceit of the spirit produces such false confidence that they can unabashedly justify and excuse themselves. Because of this they get into quarrels with other people and lapse into pride, anger, hatred, impatience, condemning, and slander. Their innocence makes them really guilty, and yet they claim to have done justly and rightly and to have acted fairly. They conceal deeply their own iniquity, for they look at their own righteousness and do not confess their sins to God sincerely and without deceit of the inner spirit. Righteous people, however, do not hide their iniquity, do not become angry, do not grow impatient even when they are wronged; for they do not feel that they can be wronged, since they find no righteousness in themselves. These are the blessed to whom God remits iniquity and cancels it because they confess it. Since they do not hide and cover their sin, God covers and hides it.[2]

- Read Matthew 18:21–35.

---

1 Bruce G. Schuchard, *1–3 John*, Concordia Commentary (St. Louis: Concordia Publishing House, 2012), 141.
2 Martin Luther, *Luther's Works*, vol. 14 (St. Louis: Concordia Publishing House, 1958), 150.

3. What does the parable say about God's willingness to forgive and the magnitude of what He is willing to forgive?

DISCUSSION NOTE: Is Peter's question really all that unreasonable? Why does Jesus point out how much the first servant owes? Is there really a limit to how much God will forgive? Who are the people in the parable meant to represent? Jesus speaks of the different ways we can respond to God's mercy. We can recognize the magnitude of our debt of sin and that the only answer is for Him to forgive us if we are to live, or we can take that forgiveness for granted. If we recognize our debt, then it stands to reason we would act accordingly. If all we are trying to do is avoid punishment, then we are not truly being grateful for what we have been given.

Peter asks Jesus an honest question about how forgiveness works, and Jesus responds with one of His helpful parables. If the master forgives a servant, and that servant is not willing to forgive another, it suggests the first servant never really thought much of that forgiveness to begin with.

In his commentary on Matthew, Dr. Jeffrey A Gibbs explains,

> Although Jesus' response makes it clear that Peter's understanding of the scope of forgiveness is inadequate, we should not fail to notice that by normal human standards, his offer to forgive a brother who sins against him up to seven times is not a trivial one. Nevertheless, whatever normal standard is guiding Peter's question is dwarfed and then swallowed up by the Christ's response.[3]

The debt owed by the first servant is such that he would have to work for a thousand years or more to pay it off. It is truly a debt that goes beyond all comprehension and yet the master, who we are meant to equate with Jesus Himself, simply forgives the debt and wipes it off the ledger. God's grace astounds us in both its quantity and quality. He forgives all sins, and

3 Jeffrey A. Gibbs, *Matthew 11:2–20:34*, Concordia Commentary (St. Louis: Concordia Publishing House, 2010), 933–34.

He forgives all sins every single time a sinner confesses them, without exception.

In the Small Catechism, Luther says, "What is Confession?" Answer: "Confession has two parts. First, that we confess our sins, and second, that we receive absolution, that is, forgiveness, from the pastor as from God Himself, not doubting, but firmly believing that by it our sins are forgiven before God in heaven" (Confession, "What is Confession?"). God forgives and is always ready to forgive. God is willing to forgive all sins, no matter what those sins are. He proves it by sending His Son to pay the debt, ensuring no sin would ever be too great to be beyond forgiveness.

That leads to a rather serious problem when we start talking about Baptism. If I can confess my sins to God and know He forgives them, just as we do in a worship service, then why do I need Baptism? Having another source of forgiveness might make sense if Absolution only covered certain sins, but God's forgiveness covers all sins, all the time. If God thought Baptism was so important that He commands us to continue doing it when we already have His forgiveness through Absolution, then perhaps it's because Baptism is doing things a bit differently. Over the next few sessions, we'll take a look at some of the events in the Bible that help us understand what Baptism is. By looking at what God has done in the past to prepare the world for Baptism, we'll see that God has some very special things going on in Baptism. When we fit all these pieces together, you'll get a glimpse of why the Church has called Baptism one of the sacred mysteries and how much God is doing for you through this gift.

Further in Depth

Luther says,

> You ask, "How does baptism help me, if it does not altogether blot out and remove sin?" This is the place for a right

> understanding of the sacrament of baptism. This blessed sacrament of baptism helps you because in it God allies himself with you and becomes one with you in a gracious covenant of comfort.
>
> In the first place you give yourself up to the sacrament of baptism and to what it signifies. That is, you desire to die, together with your sins, and to be made new at the Last Day. This is what the sacrament declares, as has been said. God accepts this desire at your hands and grants you baptism. From that hour he begins to make you a new person. He pours into you his grace and Holy Spirit, who begins to slay nature and sin, and to prepare you for death and the resurrection at the Last Day.
>
> In the second place you pledge yourself to continue in this desire, and to slay your sin more and more as long as you live, even until your dying day. This too God accepts. He trains and tests you all your life long, with many good works and with all kinds of sufferings. Thereby he accomplishes what you in baptism have desired, namely, that you may become free from sin, die, and rise again at the Last Day, and so fulfill your baptism. Therefore we read and see how bitterly he has let his saints be tortured, and how much he has let them suffer, in order that, almost slain, they might fulfill the sacrament of baptism, die, and be made new. For when this does not happen, when we do not suffer and are not tested, then the evil nature gains the upper hand so that a person invalidates his baptism, falls into sin, and remains the same old man he was before.[4]

Baptism is certainly a singular moment in a Christian's life. Coming to the font and receiving that gift of grace is a life-changing event. But that doesn't mean everything God does in Baptism begins and ends in that

4 Luther, *Luther's Works*, vol. 35 (Philadelphia: Fortress Press, 1960), 33–34.

moment. We state in the Nicene Creed, "I acknowledge one Baptism for the remission of sins." We don't get rebaptized because our Baptism has stopped working, as if we need to remind God to keep at it. Rather, we are baptized once, and that Baptism continues to work throughout the rest of our lives. It only takes a moment to be baptized, but once we are baptized, we never cease to be baptized.

That means that grace is always active. All the aspects of Baptism that we'll explore here will be at work as we continue to learn and grow as baptized children of God. We will always be sinners in this life, but that doesn't stop God from helping us to be more like the people He created us to be. This is why Luther says our Baptism is fulfilled at our death.[5] That is the point when the last vestiges of sin are wiped from our lives. "When the perishable puts on the imperishable, and the mortal puts on immortality, then shall come to pass the saying that is written: 'Death is swallowed up in victory'" (1 Corinthians 15:54). It is at this point we finally achieve the goal of Baptism—eternal life in Christ.

At a recent district pastors conference, I was asked to give a devotion on "Living in a Resurrection World." It's a topic that has a lot to do with Baptism since it is through Baptism that Christ's gift of eternal life explicitly becomes yours. Like Luther, whenever you are in doubt over what life holds or how you are going to make it through the day, you can always recall that you have been baptized. You may not know what next year, next month, or even tomorrow brings, but the end is not in doubt. Your Baptism stands as a sign and pledge to you that you have and will continue to receive everything God promises. That most assuredly means forgiveness, but it also means quite a bit more.

We'll be unpacking many of those benefits over the course of our study. For now, we simply remember that God has given us that promise and has bound Himself to us. He will never rescind that promise, for, as 1 John

5 See Luther, *Luther's Works*, vol. 36 (Philadelphia: Fortress Press, 1959), 69.

reminds us again, "He is faithful and just to forgive our sins and to cleanse us from all unrighteousness" (1:9). This is what He wants to do. He gives the Sacrament as a gift, and He enjoys giving it. Luther encourages you to be confident in your Baptism, for it is your blessed assurance that the resurrection will be yours as well. Whatever this life may throw at you, it will not be your end. It cannot be your end. You have been baptized.

Hymn Connection

"God's Own Child, I Gladly Say It"

Text by Erdmann Neumeister

This hymn makes clear that Baptism gives many benefits beyond forgiveness. Protection from temptation, protection from Satan's wiles, reassurance of God's love, and proof of our place in eternal life are all found in Baptism. The hymn connects our lives now to our lives with Christ in eternity and explains that Baptism has an integral part to play in this connection. It does not tell us how all this comes to be true, but there is only so much one hymn can do all on its own.

In this case, it is enough to see how Luther's statement connecting death to Baptism can be found elsewhere if you look. In truth, it is because of Baptism that we rightly say Christians do not enter eternal life when they die. They have already died in Christ through Baptism, so they are already living their eternal life now. Their resurrection is assured.

In Romans 6:3–4, Paul tells us, "Do you not know that all of us who have been baptized into Christ Jesus were baptized into His death? We were buried therefore with Him by baptism into death, in order that, just as Christ was raised from the dead by the glory of the Father, we too might walk in newness of life." This is a pretty major piece of baptismal theology, for it tells us that our Baptism is truly linked to the death and resurrection of Christ. His life is ours through Baptism.

Usually when this passage is referenced, it is discussed in terms of how Baptism is our spiritual death. We "die" at the font so that we may be free from the condemnation of our sin. This idea is one Luther often brings up, such as in the Small Catechism, when he says, "What does such baptizing with water indicate?" Answer:

> It indicates that the Old Adam in us should by daily contrition and repentance be drowned and die with all sins and evil desires, and that a new man should daily emerge and arise to live before God in righteousness and purity forever. (Baptism, Fourth Part)

Your Baptism is like death and is just as serious. At the same time, this hymn and the statement from Luther about death as the fulfillment of Baptism also let us think about Baptism another way. If Baptism is like death, then that also means death is like Baptism. I'm simply flipping the words around, but Paul puts the two together, allowing you to truly take it either way. It may not sound like a big deal, but it should change your whole perception of death. The hymn reminds us of the end and how we will stand before the throne of the Lamb and celebrate the victory. Your Baptism is your assurance of a place in that victory celebration. That means just as death had no hold over Christ, death also has no hold over you. It is nothing to fear. If you weren't afraid to have some water poured over your head, then you truly have no reason to fear death either. Your death will end up being just as brief and worry-free as your Baptism.

Questions for Review

Luther took great comfort in the assurance given him in Baptism. Think back to some of the crises you've faced in life.

4. Would remembering your Baptism and what it means for your eternal life have changed how you reacted at the time?

5. Might it help you keep future crises in perspective?

As I write this, the world has been in the grip of the coronavirus pandemic. Many people have been terrified of catching the disease for fear of dying. Good stewardship of ourselves and our neighbors is certainly a concern and should be something we keep in mind. At the same time, a Christian who fears death is a Christian who has forgotten his Baptism. Your resurrection is already assured, and there is nothing in this life to fear. Whether the country suffers from a pandemic, a war, or an economic crisis, or whether the issue is something you struggle with personally, remember that you are baptized. God has already seen the end of whatever it is that you are facing, and He has seen that you will come through on the other side. He has promised.

UNIT 2

THE FLOOD

As Old Testament events go, the flood isn't just one of the biggest events that relates to Baptism—it's one of the biggest events in history. Period. Luther makes it a central part of his Flood Prayer, which has continued to be a part of the Lutheran Rite of Baptism:

> Almighty and eternal God, according to Your strict judgment You condemned the unbelieving world through the flood, yet according to Your great mercy You preserved believing Noah and his family, eight souls in all.[6]

Obviously, both Baptism and the flood involve water. However, if the flood is going to tell us anything about Baptism, it has to do more than just have water. So let's take a look at the flood.

- Read Genesis 6:5–8.

1. According to God, what is the problem? What does He plan to do about it?

DISCUSSION NOTE: How many people were considered evil? To what extent is God undoing the damage caused by this evil?

2. Why does sin grieve God?

DISCUSSION NOTE: This isn't answered directly in the text. So this is

6 *LSB*, p. 268

something to consider more broadly. God says He created all of the animals and birds, as well as all mankind. Another way to ask the question, based on this idea, would be, "How can a creation offend its Creator?" That can lead to real-world parallels, such as, "How do you feel when your car breaks down?"

We don't know very much about the time after Adam and Eve. Genesis gives us a short story about Cain and Abel and then generally skips ahead to Noah. Things have gone downhill to the point that just about everyone in the world is only out for himself or herself. At this point, God seems ready to wipe everything out entirely. Luther states,

> [The evilness of man's thoughts] applies, therefore, not only to the sins before the Flood but to man's entire nature—to his heart, his reason, and his intellect, even when man feigns righteousness and wants to be most holy. This the Anabaptists do today when they get the idea into their heads that they can live without sin, and when they are intent on attaining what appear to be outstanding virtues. The rule is: When hearts are without the Holy Spirit, they do not only have no knowledge of God but even hate Him by nature. How can something that has its origin in a lack of knowledge of God and in a hatred of God be anything else than evil?[7]

It sounds pretty grim, but let's read a bit more.

- Read Genesis 6:9–7:5.

3. What is the purpose of the flood?

DISCUSSION NOTE: Is the purpose for punishment or something else? Why does God use a flood as opposed to something else? Would life in the world be different if God had not sent the flood?

7 Luther, *Luther's Works*, vol. 2 (St. Louis: Concordia Publishing House, 1960), 43.

4. **Whom is the flood directed against?**

DISCUSSION NOTE: There are other places in Scripture where God lets sin go for a long time before sending His righteous judgment. Why doesn't He let this go on longer? What does it take for God to finally decide enough is enough?

5. **Why are Noah and his family spared from the flood?**

DISCUSSION NOTE: What makes Noah and his family different from the rest of the world? What does God say about Noah? As we saw in the reading from 1 John last week, those who confess their sins are forgiven. John also says those who confess are cleansed from all unrighteousness. If God is punishing sin here, then Noah is spared because his sin is forgiven.

6. **Why do the plants and animals die in the flood too?**

DISCUSSION NOTE: Are plants and animals capable of sin? If not, why do they die? Death only comes into the world because of the sin of Adam and Eve, which shows us sin has repercussions beyond just what happens to me personally. Nothing died until sin came into the world. Now even plants and animals are subject to death.

7. **What about this passage reminds us of Baptism?**

DISCUSSION NOTE: It might be helpful to just brainstorm a bit. There aren't any wrong answers here, and the more you start thinking through what happens in the flood, the more you may see parallels to what God does in Baptism.

The flood God intends to send on the earth isn't from some desire to be cruel or vindictive. God does not delight in inflicting injury on anything in creation. He is the Creator who created this world out of love, not spite. Everything in creation was lovingly crafted to fit the niche He had specifically created for it. He is the master artist, and the universe is the canvas upon which He paints. It grieves Him when anything in His creation suffers. If we consider what it would be like if Leonardo da Vinci were forced to set fire to his Mona Lisa, we'd have some sense of what sending the flood on the world is like for God.

This is God's just and righteous judgment against sin and wickedness. Paul tells us in Romans 6:23, "For the wages of sin is death." Those who sin deserve to die. That isn't something we're comfortable hearing, and here we see God making good on that threat of punishment. Sin is the corruption of creation, destroying the good that God has made. If we consider da Vinci again, then it is like someone has come along and smeared tar across the whole canvas. The entire work is a loss except for one tiny corner da Vinci feels he can still salvage from the destruction. He could just throw the whole canvas away and start over. It would probably be easier. Instead, he chooses to put in the time and effort to save that tiny little piece because he cares about it and because he put in the work to craft it in the first place. Now the whole world is about to be washed away except for Noah's family in the ark.

It's worth noting that the flood is directed against the unrighteous people of the world, all but Noah and his family. Unfortunately, the plants and animals of the world are caught up in the same judgment. Genesis 3 shows us how mankind has an important role to play in God's creation. When men and women serve themselves instead of serving God and others, the whole order breaks down. Thorns and thistles grow where they shouldn't be growing because Adam doesn't know how to manage them anymore and his sinful nature doesn't want to manage them at all. Plants and animals are not rejecting their Creator, but they still die because of our sin.

Genesis 6:9 tells us Noah is a righteous man. Hebrews 11:7 makes clear that Noah became an "heir of the righteousness" because God warned him of what was coming, and Noah listened. Noah heeded the warning and trusted that God would save him and his family by the very means He outlined. Even though there was no evidence a flood such as God described would ever come, God's promise was enough for Noah. He trusted in that warning and promise, which is what made him and his family righteous out of all of the people on earth.

Looking at the design of Noah's ark, there are some elements (not just its size) that make it stand out from other boats. Most obvious is that there are no sails. It is not designed to catch the wind. It also does not have oars, a rudder, or anything else that might give it mobility. This boat will be designed for one simple purpose: to float. So not only is Noah building an absolutely massive boat, but he is also building a boat that is completely incapable of going anywhere. Luther remarks, "Surely, great was the faith of Noah that he was able to believe these words of God. I would certainly not have believed them."[8]

Peter describes Noah as the "herald of righteousness" (2 Peter 2:5). This suggests Noah did not shy away from telling others what God had told him in the hopes, perhaps, that they would repent and find salvation too. Unfortunately, no one else listened. God kindled faith in Noah's heart so that he was able to trust in God's warning and offer of salvation, even as the rest of the world rejected the warning and condemned themselves to death.

Luther writes,

> The Flood is truly death and the wrath of God; nevertheless, the believers are saved in the midst of the Flood. Thus death engulfs and swallows up the entire human race; for without distinction the wrath of God goes over the good and the evil, over the godly and the ungodly. The Flood that Noah experienced was not different from the one that the world experienced. The Red Sea, which both Pharaoh and Israel entered, was not different. Later on, however, the difference becomes

8 Luther, *Luther's Works*, vol. 2, 87.

> apparent in this: those who believe are preserved in the very death to which they are subjected together with the ungodly, but the ungodly perish. Noah, accordingly, is preserved because he has the ark, that is, God's promise and Word, in which he is living; but the ungodly, who do not believe the Word, are left to their fate.[9]

The whole world is baptized, but Noah and his family are the only ones to be drawn back out of the water. That's why Luther says this in the Small Catechism: "How can water do such great things?" Answer:

"Certainly not just water, but the word of God in and with the water does these things, along with the faith which trusts this word of God in the water" (Baptism, Third Part). God's word made the water of the flood a destructive, world-changing event. But Noah trusted in God's promise, so the water didn't kill him like it did the rest of the world. God spoke, and Noah believed.

God's judgment rains down a number of times in the Old Testament. Several of these instances you may know well, such as the flood, when God sends fire down upon Sodom and Gomorrah for their blatant disregard for anyone but themselves, or when He sends the final plague on Egypt to wipe out the firstborn males of the land. In each case, God shows the extent to which He will destroy sin in the land. His judgment hits the land like a hammer, striking it until it shatters and the sin is finally put away or removed. However, in each case, those who trust in Him are saved from the devastation. Death falls all around, but those who look to Him for protection are kept safe.

Through the flood, God sought to wipe away the unrepentant sin from the land. The whole world experiences this washing of the water. The water is deadly and brings destruction everywhere, but not for Noah. Noah trusts

9 Luther, *Luther's Works*, vol. 2, 153.

in God, so the water has no judgment to give there. Where water brings death everywhere else, for Noah it brings new life and a new world to step out into. It is as fresh and pure as anything can be prior to the resurrection.

- Read 1 Peter 3:18–22.

8. What did Noah receive through the waters of the flood?

DISCUSSION NOTE: Consider why God waited for Noah to finish the ark. God could have brought that judgment against sin anytime. He chose to wait for Noah.

The rest of life on earth died, but not Noah. In a figurative sense, Noah rose from the dead, much like Jesus would later do. This isn't the only place the Bible talks this way. I mentioned Hebrews 11:7 a few pages back. This passage describes exemplars of the faith, notably Noah and Abraham. The author of Hebrews tells us Abraham also received Isaac back from the dead when he was called upon to sacrifice his son. God meant what He said when He commanded Abraham to sacrifice His son, and Abraham listened and followed through until God stopped him. Noah is described as someone who, in reverent fear, built the ark to save his household from a threat he had no evidence would ever come. Both men trusted in God's promise and were saved from death by listening to Him. God is teaching us a bit about what Jesus would later demonstrate through His own death and resurrection. In the next unit, we'll look more at the implications of what Noah experienced:

> That water drowned everything that had life. Thus Baptism drowns everything that is carnal and natural; it makes spiritual men. But we take ship in the ark, which represents the Lord Christ, or the Christian Church, or the Gospel which Christ preaches, or the body of Christ to which we cling through faith; and we are saved, just as Noah was saved in the ark. Thus you see that the analogy summarizes what faith and the

> cross, life and death, are. Now where there are people who cling to Christ, there a Christian Church is sure to be. There everything that comes from Adam and is evil is drowned.[10]

Sin is judged, and all that remains is righteousness. The world is washed clean, and the stain of sin is removed. Noah was saved from death because he trusted in God to save him. God provided the means of escaping the devastation. By trusting that God would uphold His promise, Noah lives through the punishment of death that was dealt out to the whole world and comes out on the other side unscathed.

Further in Depth

The flood already shows us some very important connections to Baptism. We'll continue looking at themes that will reinforce what we have already seen here, but some of those themes are already coming out quite strongly. Noah's trust in God turned aside the worldwide destruction, a tiny bubble of life in a world covered in watery death.

While everything we've looked at so far broadens our understanding of what Baptism does for us now, there are also some important things to remember here and as we continue through our study of baptismal themes in the Old Testament. The first is that the flood may tell us about Baptism, but the flood is not actually Baptism. This is one of those statements I'll make that may sound obvious, but it bears consideration. God did send the flood to wipe out the unrighteous people across the land. God granted Noah the power to trust His ominous pronouncement of the impending flood. Noah built the ark, gathered his family and the animals, and was saved, just as God promised. The rest of the world perished in its sin.

This might suggest that Noah is now free from sin since he survived the flood that came to wipe sin away from creation. But Noah is still very

10 Luther, *Luther's Works*, vol. 30 (St. Louis: Concordia Publishing House, 1967), 115–16.

much a sinner. He still grows old and dies, just like anyone else. The flood has much to teach us about Baptism. It shows us the extent to which God will go to wipe out sin. It shows us how even in an event that wipes out quite literally everyone else on the planet, God can and will save those who trust in Him. However, God never promises He will wipe away Noah's sin with the flood. That isn't what the flood was ever meant to do.

Back at the beginning of the unit, we saw how Luther connected the flood to Baptism. Just as foreshadowing in a book is intended to prepare you for when the real event comes, the flood prepares us for Baptism. The flood could never serve the purpose of Baptism, for full and complete salvation can only be found in Christ. Until the coming of Christ, no event in history has the power to offer anything more than temporary safety. The Early Church theologian Tertullian wrote quite a bit on Baptism. He speaks to this as well:

> For just as, after the waters of the deluge, by which the old iniquity was purged—after the baptism, so to say, of the world—a *dove* was the herald which announced to the earth the assuagement of celestial wrath, when she had been sent her way out of the ark, and had returned with the olive-branch, a sign which even among the nations is the fore-token of *peace;* so by the self-same law of heavenly effect, to earth—that is, to our flesh—as it emerges from the font, after its old sins, flies the *dove* of the Holy Spirit, bringing us the peace of God, sent out from the heavens, where is the Church, the typified ark. But the world returned unto sin; in which point baptism would ill be compared to the deluge. And so it is destined to fire; just as the man too is, who after baptism renews his sins: so that this also ought to be accepted as a sign for our admonition.[11]

11 Tertullian, "On Baptism," in *The Ante-Nicene Fathers: The Writings of the Fathers down to AD 32*, vol. 3 (Grand Rapids, MI: Eerdmans, 1957), 673.

Tertullian says a lot about the Holy Spirit here. We'll get to Him a bit later in our study. Right now we are more interested in how Tertullian points out that the world returned to sin. If we were to continue reading Genesis, we'd see that it is not all that long after Noah leaves the ark and his family resettles the land that we have the tower of Babel incident. God does not wipe out the people here, but He does take pretty drastic action to thwart their sinful endeavors.

The flood has come and gone for Noah. Many unbelievers were wiped out, but sin is not gone for good. Not yet. For that to happen, God needs to do something even bigger and more sweeping. There are many other elements that need to come together to make that possible. This is why the flood and every other work God does on behalf of His people ultimately points us to Christ. He will be the one to bring all this together and give it purpose.

Hymn Connection

"Great Is Thy Faithfulness"

Text by Thomas O. Chisholm

The lyrics to this hymn do not specifically refer to the flood or to the beginning of creation. What they do refer to is the long-standing work of God in the midst of creation. Whether during the flood or any other disaster, God still keeps His promises. Creation itself bears witness to how God provides for His faithful people even when it looks like nothing could possibly save them. The time Noah spent building the ark, surviving the storm, and then waiting for the waters to subside is a testimony to how God keeps them safe in both the short term and over the long haul.

Questions for Review

9. What does God say about the lengths He will go to in order to wipe out sin?

10. Think about Noah as he hears God tell him to build an ark for the upcoming disaster. If you had been in his position, how do you think you would have responded?

11. Consider also the nature of the flood. If God can provide for Noah in the midst of a disaster that wipes out all that moves on the ground, is there truly anything He can't protect you from?

God's devastation of all that lived on the dry land is complete and total. This already tells us something about how God views sin. No amount of sin can be tolerated in God's good creation. Noah does not quite arrive in a completely new and sinless world, for he himself still has sin. However, this still shows us something about what God will do later when it is time to fully inaugurate God's new world. As for our response to God's declaration, it's hard to see how any of us would take such a statement very seriously. Even Luther admits such an announcement is beyond belief. The fact that Noah hears and believes is an expression of exactly how faith works. In spite of the lack of immediate evidence, God grants us the ability to trust Him and find salvation. Truly, if God can save Noah from a disaster like this, there is nothing God cannot save you from.

UNIT 3

Creation

Noah's experience of the flood is quite profound. Life on earth is washed away, but Noah and his family remain. Judgment falls, but they are spared. Noah gets his life back. That, all by itself, tells us something about what God will do later through water and His Word. But as far back in history as the flood was, it was already looking further back to events that had come before it. Let's take a look.

- Read Genesis 1:1–2:3.

1. **What is the first thing to exist in all creation?**

DISCUSSION NOTE: Look carefully at the text. Obviously, God is not created. He is the Creator, and that holds true regardless of whether you are talking about God the Father, Son, or Holy Spirit. When looking at the first day, we usually look at the first thing the text tells us God does. However, if you look carefully, you'll see there is something there already. Before God speaks light into creation, He has already been busy creating.

2. **What significant things are taking place on the second and third days?**

DISCUSSION NOTE: It looks as though God is preparing creation for the appearance of plants and animals. For those to be there, they need a place to live. If that's true, then why does God need to do what He does on the second day?

3. What are the parameters God uses in His creation of man?

DISCUSSION NOTE: We'll get into a lot of this in more detail later on. For now it's worth just talking through how God makes Adam and Eve different and distinct from the rest of creation. Talk through what it means to be made in the "image of God." Is it a physical image or something else, and how do you know?

4. What event completes God's creative work?

DISCUSSION NOTE: God's rest on the seventh day isn't work, per se, but it is still an important part of the process. God ceases His work of creation because there is nothing more to add. It is complete. This isn't to say God is passively watching creation now. He is still busy maintaining it, but the work of creation is done for now, and He has provided everything it needs.

5. Which persons of the Trinity are involved in creation?

DISCUSSION NOTE: The Father is usually considered the Creator since that's how we describe Him in the Creeds. "I believe in God, the Father Almighty, maker of heaven and earth." The Spirit is pretty clearly here as well. Does Jesus get left out here? If the group identifies different persons of the Trinity, ask what each is doing here.

The whole work of creation is something we learn about as Christians, but rarely do we dig into some of the details that God has hidden there. Creation is very much a trinitarian work. Right from the very beginning, the triune God is fully involved in His new creation. We typically think of light as the first thing God makes, and it is certainly the highlight of the first day, but we see the Spirit hovering over this formless ball of water, the first thing God makes and the substance He uses to build the rest of our world. The Father oversees all this activity. But rather than molding the world with His hands, building and shaping every rock and tree as one might make a diorama, the Father simply speaks. The Gospel of John tells us this is where we find the Son, the Word by whom all things were made.

The Father speaks, and that message, that Word, is Christ Himself. This work of the Trinity will be an important connection later as we examine Baptism. For now, it tells us how involved each person is in the work of creation.

The third day brings plants into God's creation, but before that, God divides the waters into those above and those below. Already we are setting the stage for what we'll see later in the flood. Scripture doesn't tell us what the purpose of this division is. It tells us simply that God determined that it needed to happen to make the world habitable.

The creation of Adam and Eve is an event that has been the focus of a great many theological debates. God creates man "in His own image" (Genesis 1:27). The word *image* is not meant in a physical sense here but in a spiritual and metaphorical sense. As God picks up a clump of earth and molds the first man, He creates that man to be in a relationship with Him. For that to happen, that man must be perfect, for God's presence cannot allow sin without destroying it utterly. As a perfect man, Adam trusts God implicitly and thus carries God's own righteousness. Because Adam is perfect, there is nothing broken in him that could lead to his body's breakdown and eventual death. Adam is in the image of God because he reflects God's love right back to Him.

When Adam sins, he loses that image because he is no longer able to reflect God's love back to Him. Adam is filled with love for himself instead of love for others. With that sin, God's created order breaks down, and now everything is subject to decay, disorder, and death. Adam was created in the image of God, but he lost it through his own sinful choice. Now, if Adam is to be restored to the image he was created to have, God must bring about that restoration.

Before Adam's sin, God completes His work by resting on the seventh day and marking it as a holy day of rest. The whole world falls into this system of seven days making up a week and then repeating. God created the world to work that way, and we all naturally fall into that rhythm.

Before we continue looking at creation, let's put some pieces together.

- Read Genesis 9:7–17.

6. What are the terms of the covenant God establishes with Noah?

DISCUSSION NOTE: It's helpful to know what a *covenant* is. The word is roughly equivalent to a contract. A covenant is made between two or more groups and is considered binding on those who are a part of it. There are two main types of covenants found in Scripture. A two-sided contract requires both groups to do something to fulfill the covenant. If either side fails to fulfill their part of the bargain, then the punishments outlined in the covenant come into effect. Other covenants are one-sided. One group offers to do something, and the other group is not required to do anything in return. Which type of covenant is God establishing with Noah? What does it require?

7. Who is the rainbow for? What is its purpose?

DISCUSSION NOTE: The usual thought is that the rainbow reminds us of God's grace in saving Noah and other righteous people from His judgment against sin. It can certainly do that, and God gives us reminders of His love and grace constantly, but that isn't the primary purpose of the rainbow here. The rainbow fits in as part of the covenant God establishes, not just with Noah but with the whole world.

8. What is the command God gives Noah and his family?

DISCUSSION NOTE: It might be obvious, but it is worth recalling where this command came up before: back in Genesis 1 after God created Adam and Eve. God gave this command back when the world was perfect and sinless. He gives it again to remind them the command is still there.

In order to answer the questions, we must put ourselves in the place of

Noah. He climbs into the ark with his family and all the animals. God shuts the door. Then it starts to rain. The people die. The animals and plants die. Dry land disappears. The sun, moon, and stars disappear. Genesis 7:11 tells us, "On that day all the fountains of the great deep burst forth, and the windows of the heavens were opened." The waters God had separated on the third day come together again. Under forty days of rain, God rewinds the days of creation as even light is more or less erased under the dark storm clouds.

When the rain finally ceases, Noah looks out over the side of the ark and sees nothing but water stretching unbroken to the horizon in every direction. It is almost as if he is there at the very beginning of creation where nothing exists but the water God will use to build the rest of the world. Then, slowly, all the things God made start to return. The dark, angry storm clouds calm and allow light to trickle through. Eventually, they part, and the heavenly bodies are visible in the sky. Dry land appears, and the ark finally comes to rest. Then the world is filled once more with plants, animals, and people.

God calls to mind the command He gave Adam and Eve back in Genesis 1:28: "Be fruitful and multiply and fill the earth and subdue it, and have dominion over the fish of the sea and over the birds of the heavens and over every living thing that moves on the earth." Noah walks out of the ark into a world that closely resembles the world of Genesis 1. It is as if God had wound back time and reset the world through the flood. The unrighteous people have been washed away, and the world has been made clean once more.

Sin is not completely gone, but God tells us something about what He does with water. The world is re-created through the flood. Noah trusted in God, and his trust was not in vain. Like Abraham later on, Noah trusted and was counted as righteous because he was saved from judgment. The flood waters came in judgment, but Noah was saved and not destroyed. Noah need never face this kind of judgment again, for he is already righteous. God puts the rainbow in the sky, not for Noah but for Himself. From this time forward, whenever God looks down at Noah, He'll see the rainbow and remember Noah has already been judged and found innocent.

In the same way, our Baptism protects us and is a constant reminder to God that we have already been washed clean and made righteous. We trust in God and come to the font, knowing that He'll wash our sins away and that our trust is not in vain. It also means we have been re-created and restored to our original state of righteousness in the eyes of God. We have been given the image of God once more. We'll take a closer look at what that means in the next unit.

For now, let's back up a bit and look at one more section.

- Read Genesis 7:6–8:12.

9. What are the different time frames listed here? Are those times significant? If so, how?

DISCUSSION NOTE: Genesis 7:11 gives a date relative to Noah's life for when the flood finally comes. This is not a "once upon a time" kind of story. This is related as an actual historical event that Noah has certainly marked on his calendar. Nothing in this story is meant to be taken figuratively. Perhaps more significantly are the numbers *7* and *40* that show up here. Where else do we find these numbers? Is there a connection between them?

10. What, if anything, is significant about the creatures that show up in this section of text?

DISCUSSION NOTE: Like the previous question, both ravens and doves show up elsewhere in Scripture. The raven isn't very successful here, so that may not be as strong of a connection as the dove. Where else do we see a dove?

Things that get repeated in various places in Scripture are not always related. However, when you see something show up more than once, such as the number *7*, it's worth at least investigating to see if they are connected somehow. This sort of repetition isn't usually something you want to put too much weight on unless the text specifically says why it's important, but it often works as circumstantial evidence. Enough circumstantial evidence eventually adds up to a pretty strong connection. I'm not going to unpack all these things at this point because we need to explore some other ideas first before these puzzle pieces will fit. But we need to at least mark them down so we remember where they came from.

First is the number *7*. This should already be making us think of creation, and rightly so. We've already seen how the flood is a restoration of God's initial work in creation. However, Genesis 7:10 says the rain began not on the seventh day but *after* the seventh day. That makes the number not *7*, but *7 + 1*, or *8*. This number will actually show up more than once in Scripture and will play a rather important role in our understanding of Baptism. The number *7* also shows up in chapter 8 as Noah tests things with some birds to see if life has returned to earth. Perhaps a reinforcement of the creation theme as God is busy restoring the world as the waters subside.

The number *40* also shows up here a couple times. It shows up in Genesis 7:17 and then again in 8:6. Genesis 8:6 suggests a time of waiting—forty days that Noah has been waiting for things to begin to return to normal. Genesis 7:17 tells us the rain fell for forty days. God inflicted His wrath against sin on the world for forty days. In either case, we see the number *40* show up in Scripture in a couple of other significant places, such as the number of days Jesus spent in the wilderness being tempted after His Baptism. We also see it as the number of years the Israelites spent in the wilderness before entering the Promised Land. Both of these will come up again in our study.

Finally, the dove comes into play. Doves don't show up much in Scripture. The most noteworthy place is, of course, Jesus' own Baptism. This also suggests something important and worth looking into. All these pieces have a common thread: Baptism. None of them are enough to base a lot on all by themselves, but looking at how and where they connect will add further weight to the idea that everything going on back here with creation and the flood is really meant to tell us about what God will be doing later in Baptism.

Further in Depth

Studying the flood and creation gives us the opportunity to talk about the "now/not yet" concept that runs through the New Testament. As Jesus says in John 15, He and His disciples are not of the world. We are always looking for the new creation that is to come when He returns in glory. We know at that point that sin will be wiped away forever and we will enjoy perfect peace. That peace can't exist in this world because we and the world are still tainted by sin.

The perfect joy and peace that awaits us with the return of Christ and the resurrection of all flesh is something all Christians eagerly look forward to. At the end of Revelation, Jesus says, "Surely I am coming soon." John and the whole Church reply, "Amen. Come, Lord Jesus!" (22:20). We constantly pray for Christ to return and bring a full and final end to sin, death, and Satan because they still torment God's people.

Though we are waiting for the day when sin will be completely gone, we also know Christ has already died for our sins and forgives those sins now. Luther speaks to this in his discussion of Confession in the Small Catechism:

> What is Confession? Confession has two parts. First, that

> we confess our sins, and second, that we receive absolution, that is forgiveness, from the pastor as from God Himself, not doubting, but firmly believing that by it our sins are forgiven before God in heaven. (Confession, "What is Confession?")

We are looking for what God has promised to do for us in the future, but God is also already at work in the world now. Even though we are still living with sin in our lives because Christ hasn't returned, we are already seen as sinless by Him because the sins we have are forgiven.

This idea extends to just about every other aspect of our lives, as well as the lives of those who have come before us. Baptism works similarly here. As we look back to Noah, we can see how the flood showed him a bit of what was to come. The flood looked forward to a washing that would cleanse not just the surface but the inside as well, namely Baptism. Though the Sacrament of Baptism did not exist in Noah's day, God was still at work in his life. Noah still saw God's salvation as He saved him from physical death and still acknowledged him as righteous.

Noah stepped out of the ark into a world that resembled the world God had first created, but it still bore the taint of sin. Noah looked forward to a world that would truly be free of sin. But even with the flood, it had not arrived yet. Baptism would do more than the flood did since it brings spiritual cleansing, but it still doesn't solve the problem of sin in the world completely either. Luther also says of Baptism in the Small Catechism,

> What does such baptizing with water indicate? It indicates that the Old Adam in us should by daily contrition and repentance be drowned and die with all sins and evil desires, and that a new man should daily emerge and arise to live before God in righteousness and purity forever. (Baptism, Fourth Part)

Hymn Connection

"Joyful, Joyful We Adore Thee"

Text by Henry Van Dyke

Psalm 8:3–4 says, "When I look at Your heavens, the work of Your fingers, the moon and the stars, which You have set in place, what is man that You are mindful of him, and the son of man that You care for him?" Psalm 19:1–2 says, "The heavens declare the glory of God, and the sky above proclaims His handiwork. Day to day pours out speech, and night to night reveals knowledge." In both cases, the psalmist reflects on the wonders of creation. God has made the world and everything in it. Everything He makes reflects who He is and bears His stamp. Adam and Eve may not have realized how wondrous the world was when they took their first steps in the Garden of Eden, but they probably thought about it quite a bit after they were sent out from it. The world still proclaimed the glory of its Creator to the best of its ability, but it had a much more difficult time doing so.

Noah sees a glimpse of this as he steps out of the ark, and for the moment, everything looks pristine. The world is as close to perfection as creation can be with sin still running through it. The joy that filled creation as God's creatures entered into it once more, having survived their baptismal flood, was assuredly a thing to behold. Noah and all creation now bore witness to a mighty act of God and proof that He saves His people even when judgment falls on the entire rest of the world. Noah and all living things would look in awe at the rainbow that filled the skies and know with certainty they had received God's great mercy.

Questions for Review

11. **As you're going about your life over the week, take a moment to consider some of the everyday things you come across.**

What would they be like if you were able to take them back to the garden before the fall into sin?

12. Would they work or act differently? If so, how? Consider how much your life would change if everything around you worked perfectly like it would have in the garden.

We tend to think of many things as normal simply because they happen all the time. Cats scratch people. Dogs bite. Gusting storms knock down tree limbs that damage power lines and houses. Spiders scare people. Cars break down. All these issues are a part of the fallen world. Cats, dogs, spiders, and winds all existed in the garden, yet they did none of those things. Cars, perhaps, also would have existed in time but never would have broken down. That makes all those problems very abnormal, at least as God sees them. Every aspect of this world is tainted by sin, but we rarely think about it because that's the only world we know. Nearly everything in the world would operate very, very differently if sin were no longer a factor. We don't know exactly what life in God's new creation will look like, but we do know it will have the same kind of perfection Adam and Eve knew before sin came into the world. The few glimpses we are given in Scripture of the new creation show a world that reflects that same kind of pristine life that once existed so long ago.

UNIT 4

The Image of God

The image of God isn't just a matter of who you are but also what you do. Adam and Eve were created in God's own righteousness, which meant they had jobs to do in the world where God had placed them. God has already given them a command in Genesis 1:28. Let's take a look again.

- Read Genesis 1:26–30.

1. What are Adam and Eve supposed to do?

DISCUSSION NOTE: We've discussed Genesis 1–2 before, but now we are specifically looking at the command God gave to Adam and Eve. This command tells them they have a job to do in the world. The world is perfect, but there is still work to be done. It might sound like God is giving two commands in Genesis 1:28, but one leads to the other. Plants and animals are spreading around the world, so the world needs more people to help manage it.

Aside from being fruitful and multiplying, Adam and Eve were supposed to manage the world God had given them. This doesn't mean God had abandoned His supervision of the world. It was more like He involved Adam and Eve in His work. God built the rules for how the world would work. He allowed Adam and Eve to manage things within that system. Luther says a bit more:

> Here [in Gen. 1:26] the rule is assigned to the most beautiful

> creature, who knows God and is the image of God, in whom the similitude of the divine nature shines forth through his enlightened reason, through his justice and his wisdom. Adam and Eve become the rulers of the earth, the sea, and the air. . . . Adam and Eve heard the words with their ears when God said: "Have dominion." Therefore the naked human being—without weapons and walls, even without any clothing, solely in his bare flesh—was given the rule over all birds, wild beasts, and fish.[12]

Adam and Eve carry the authority of the Creator as they tend to the world around them. God makes the flowers grow, but Adam and Eve are given the authority to tell them where to grow. But with the loss of the image of God, this job becomes more difficult. Let's take a look at what dominion looks like now.

- Read Genesis 3:17–19.

2. What does this dominion look like in a fallen world?

DISCUSSION NOTE: We can take some educated guesses about what life would have been like in the world before sin. How would our interactions with plants and animals change if we didn't have sin in the way? What sorts of problems do we face as we take care of the world now that Adam and Eve wouldn't have had to deal with?

Adam and Eve still have the job, but nothing works like it is intended to anymore. Where once they might have laid out orderly orchards and flower beds and known everything would grow exactly where they wanted, now the connection between God and creation, which flows through mankind, is broken, and creation grows wild and unmanaged.

In general, Baptism is the means by which God returns us to that original image and righteousness we once had, but Scripture also tells us more

12 Luther, *Luther's Works*, vol. 1 (St. Louis: Concordia Publishing House, 1958), 66.

about how important Baptism is to this restoration. Now let's look at how God starts to bring us back into that position:

- Read 1 Samuel 16:1–13.

3. Who receives the anointing here?

DISCUSSION NOTE: This is pretty straightforward, but we need to understand who this person is before we can understand why the anointing is important.

4. What is the purpose of the anointing?

DISCUSSION NOTE: It may be helpful to ask more generally what the purpose of anointing is and then ask what it is being used for here. The end of the passage says the Spirit rushes on David, and it might sound like that's what his anointing was for, but verse 1 tells us why Samuel is being sent. Israel needs a new king, and God has chosen David to fill that role.

Samuel takes the oil and pours it on the head of David, and now David is marked as king over Israel. Saul had initially been chosen to be the first king of Israel. Unfortunately, it didn't take Saul long to follow his own path. He stopped listening to God and opted instead to do things his own way. Saul disqualified himself from the position of king.

So God chooses David to replace him. David is anointed here, announcing that God has chosen him and will establish him as king. David lives as a shepherd now and has very little experience in leading armies or ruling a nation, so God gives him time to learn the ropes before he takes on the job. He may not be officially ruling yet, but God has named him king, so it is a foregone conclusion that it will come to pass. Soon, Saul will be removed and David will take his place on the throne as king. It may seem rather strange to use oil to mark a king, but oil has a very special purpose in the life of God's people.

- Read Exodus 30:22–33.

5. What does God say is the purpose of this oil?

DISCUSSION NOTE: Similarly to the previous question about anointing, it might be helpful to hear what people think about the use of oil in general. Some church denominations, even some LCMS churches, will use oil to anoint those who are sick or injured. Some denominations, like Catholic and Orthodox, will do "chrismation," which is an anointing they see as working in conjunction with Baptism. In this text, it is specifically related to the concept of holiness.

6. What does it mean to be made holy?

DISCUSSION NOTE: This is another question aimed at something the participants may have heard but probably haven't thought much about. The word *holy* shows up in many places connected with the Church. "Holy Bible," "Holy Baptism," "Holy Communion," "Holy Christian Church," and last but not least, "Holy Spirit." We use the word over and over again without a good sense of what we are talking about. The Bible isn't just a book—it is a holy book. Baptism, a word that comes from Greek and simply means "to wash," is not just a simple washing like one might get in a shower. It is a holy washing. Communion isn't a meal like one might share with family or friends. It is a holy meal. Likewise, the Church and the Spirit are different than other organizations, gods, or spirits in the world. In all this, *holy* means something "is set apart and distinct from the rest."

7. Why couldn't anyone else use this oil?

DISCUSSION NOTE: Anyone could use any other oil they might want. Lamp oil or perfume oil was all perfectly acceptable for anyone to use, as long as it wasn't *this* oil. This oil was God's and was meant only for God's purposes. It had to be used by His rules if it was going to accomplish the task as it was intended.

The anointing oil is used for pouring over many things. Most of the items used for ritual service to God, such as the furnishings of the tabernacle and all the utensils, are anointed with this oil. This marks them as holy—given to and claimed by God. This is why God alone uses the oil. He doesn't want anyone else to be confused about what its purpose is. The things (or people) anointed with this oil are His and will always be His. They are not to be used for mundane purposes anymore.

In this particular case, Aaron and his sons are being anointed. We'll look a bit more at them in the next unit. For now, we can see the purpose here. Whatever Aaron might have been before, now he is anointed and given to God to be put to work in His service to bring His grace to the people. Aaron is different than the man he was before. He is no longer his own person. He must think and act like a representative of God and know that the things he does, whether good or bad, will reflect on God as well.

In that way, Aaron was reflecting God's own Son, Jesus Christ. In His Baptism, Jesus was anointed with the Holy Spirit, set apart as God's perfect representative. "He is the radiance of the glory of God and the exact imprint of His nature, and He upholds the universe by the word of His power" (Hebrews 1:3). Or as Jesus said about His ministry, "Do you not believe that I am in the Father and the Father is in Me? The words that I say to you I do not speak on My own authority, but the Father who dwells in Me does His works" (John 14:10).

There's a reason the Church has always referred to the Sacrament as "Holy Baptism." When Jesus tells His disciples to baptize "in the name of the Father and of the Son and of the Holy Spirit" (Matthew 28:19), it tells us that God is, in essence, putting His stamp of ownership on that person baptized, just as the oil of anointing did in the days of the Israelites.

To be baptized, then, is to be restored to the original state of kingship mankind was meant to have—the same kingship Adam had. Luther says,

> And again, the situation of Adam, as the initiator of sin, was worse than ours, if we appraise it correctly. Where we work hard, each one in his own station, Adam was compelled to

> exert himself in the hard work of the household, of the state, and of the church all by himself. As long as he lived, he alone held all these positions among his descendants. He supported his family, ruled it, and trained it in godliness; he was father, king, and priest. And experience teaches how each one of these positions abounds in grief and dangers.[13]

In the Old Testament, kings were made by anointing. Jesus was made King of kings and Lord of lords at His Baptism when He was anointed with the Holy Spirit. New Testament kings are made by Baptism. Adam and Eve were to have dominion over the world, serving as king and queen under the King of kings. This was the position and duty they gave up when they tried to go beyond their creaturely limitations and have something more. Now God restores us to that role and gives us the ability to look beyond ourselves to the world around us and see how it is ours to care for and protect. Let's look at the other two classes of people who receive anointing and how they relate to us.

As we saw, anointing was God's way of showing the world what was His. The role of king was one Adam and Eve had from the very beginning, but kings aren't the only ones who are anointed. Let's go back and take another look at Aaron.

- Read Leviticus 8:1–10, 30–36.

8. What is the purpose of the anointing?

DISCUSSION NOTE: Take a look at what happens here and what happens in 1 Samuel 16, where David is anointed king. What is the same? What is different?

9. Why does Aaron receive this anointing?

DISCUSSION NOTE: When God calls to Moses out of the burning bush, He

13 Luther, *Luther's Works*, vol. 1, 213–14.

tells Moses to go to Pharaoh and tell him to let the Israelites go out into the wilderness where they can worship Him.

10. What is the time frame over which this ordination takes place?

DISCUSSION NOTE: God likes to repeat themes in Scripture. Often when you see a number repeated, there is something there worth paying attention to. You might ask the participants if they can think of places where certain numbers get repeated. The number *12* is used for the number of tribes of Israel as well as the number of disciples. It rains for forty days while Noah is on the ark, and Jesus is in the wilderness forty days before being tempted by Satan. The number *7* gets used a lot, starting with creation. Think through other places you see numbers repeated.

11. What is significant about this time frame?

DISCUSSION NOTE: Take a look at the different connections you made in the previous question and think about whether God is trying to communicate something here. If so, what?

This is quite an involved chapter. Aaron puts on all the vestments of priesthood, and Moses offers sacrifices on Aaron's behalf. The anointing seen here accomplishes the same thing for Aaron as we learned it did for King David. In this case, God is not claiming Aaron as a king but as a priest. Aaron will have a special role in the work of God's grace and forgiveness. Aaron will act as the go-between, speaking God's words of forgiveness to the people and offering their gifts back to Him.

Earlier in this unit, we saw Luther comment on how Adam was both a king and a priest. Adam was meant to order and organize creation, but he was also meant to be the connecting point between God and the rest of the world. As he turned his attention on himself and not on God or the world, he gave up this role as well. Now this connection is severed and the world is full of sin. For God to exist in a sinful world without destroying it outright, He must cleanse pieces of it so He can be here without hurting us.

This is why the tabernacle and all its furnishings are anointed and consecrated to God's service. They won't be sullied by mundane use that might prevent them from serving as tools for God's grace. Aaron, too, is anointed and claimed by God. He is not to sully himself with worldly things anymore. If he is too corrupted by worldly sins that he no longer sees his position as important, then God's people lose that connection to their Creator.

In 1 Peter 2:5, Peter declares that the Church is "a spiritual house, to be a holy priesthood, to offer spiritual sacrifices acceptable to God through Jesus Christ." He echoes the declaration God made to the Israelites and now applies it to us. What Aaron does and what Adam was meant to do was intended to be something the whole nation participated in. What Aaron did for the Israelites was something all the Israelites were supposed to be doing for the rest of the world. They were supposed to be bringing the concerns of the world to God and sharing what God says about those things. They fell into heathen religions and gave up that role. The holy priesthood is critical to the working of God's grace and for the care of the people. So God removed the Israelites as His people and found a new group of people to fill the role: the Church.

The ordination of Aaron takes place over seven days, and he begins his service on the eighth. This number should make us think of the days of creation. God takes seven days to complete the work of creation. In that work of creation, Adam and Eve are made in the image of God. With the loss of the image of God, God anoints Aaron and, in a sense, re-creates him by sending him through that creation all over again. This is similar to the sense we get from Noah and the flood as well. Aaron is put back into the role Adam once had. Luther says further,

> After God has given man the administration of government and of the home, has set him up as king of the creatures, and has added the tree of life as a safeguard for preserving this physical life, He now builds him, as it were, a temple that he

> may worship Him and thank the God who has so kindly bestowed all these things on him. Today in our churches we have an altar for the administration of the Eucharist, and we have platforms or pulpits for teaching the people. These objects were built not only to meet a need but also to create a solemn atmosphere. But this tree of the knowledge of good and evil was Adam's church, altar, and pulpit. Here he was to yield to God the obedience he owed, give recognition to the Word and will of God, give thanks to God, and call upon God for aid against temptation.[14]

Aaron is made a priest again through this anointing, which prefigures Jesus' Baptism, when He was anointed as our High Priest. God achieves the same result in us through Holy Baptism. We, too, are brought back into the priesthood and given the duty of being the go-between for God and the rest of the world.

The anointing of priests and kings is significant all on its own, but those are not the only people God anoints.

- Read 1 Kings 19:9–18.

12. Who does God direct Elijah to anoint? What roles do they serve?

DISCUSSION NOTE: Several passages from Elijah's ministry turn up in the regular readings of the Church Year, depending on whether you follow the one-year or three-year lectionaries. Many are taught in Sunday School as well. Elijah's ministry begins as he predicts a drought in Israel as a result of the idolatry of the people, especially King Ahab. He stays with a poor foreign widow and her son during this time. He ensures they have food during the drought and brings the boy back to life after he suddenly passes away. A while later, Elijah faces off against many false prophets, and God proves He truly is God by consuming Elijah's sacrifice with fire, while the false prophets find their sacrifice left untouched. After this, Elijah runs

14 Luther, *Luther's Works*, vol. 1, 94–95.

away in fear of King Ahab and Queen Jezebel. After God reminds him He is there with him, He sends him out to continue the work he needs to do.

We've seen kings anointed already. So, it is no surprise that Elijah would be directed to anoint kings here. However, prophets are new to us. As theirs is another position that's important to the functioning of God's people, it shouldn't surprise us that prophets would be ordained as well. But what is it that makes someone a prophet? Let's take a look.

- Read Deuteronomy 18:15–22.

13. How would you know if someone is a prophet?

DISCUSSION NOTE: One way to approach this question is to identify what makes prophets, priests, and kings distinct. Kings bring order to the world that has been put into their care. Priests act on behalf of the world in carrying their concerns to God. Prophets primarily act in the other direction—sharing God's Word with the world.

14. What is prophecy?

DISCUSSION NOTE: Some church bodies will talk about prophecy quite a bit. They will often describe this among the main gifts of the Spirit, such as speaking in tongues and miraculous healing. You might ask what your participants have heard from other denominations. Compare this to what comes to mind when talking about some of the better-known biblical prophets, like Elijah, Moses, or Isaiah.

15. Are there prophets in the world today?

DISCUSSION NOTE: Prophets are sent to speak God's Word. That doesn't necessarily mean they proclaim something new. In fact, many of the prophets sent to Israel in the Old Testament are saying the same thing over and over: judgment is coming because of their persistent idolatry. Paul warns against those who preach "a different gospel" (Galatians 1:8) because there is no such thing. God has given us everything we need to know for salvation and eternal life. But prophecy isn't about telling the future. So the question is, Are there people in the world today who proclaim God's Word?

Looking back on the life of Moses and of the prophets that will come after him, God describes what makes someone a prophet. We tend to think of prophecy as just telling the future, but there's a subtle distinction here. Prophets aren't really interested in telling the future. They are there to proclaim God's Word. Because the messages proclaimed by God's prophets are His, they must come to pass. Whether the Word to be proclaimed is one of salvation or judgment, the prophet's job is the same.

The list of those individuals God called specifically to be prophets ended with John the Baptist. When Jesus was anointed with the Holy Spirit in His Baptism, Jesus took His place as prophet supreme. Though the biblical role of prophet has ended, Christians are still called to be prophets in their lives today. With the completion of Scripture, there is nothing new to be revealed to God's people before Christ returns. In that sense, prophets are no longer necessary. However, as Christians, we are still called to proclaim the Word God has revealed. God told us much about the future regarding the new creation and the work He has yet to complete. He has promised it to His people, and His promise will be fulfilled. That means we still have work to do proclaiming what God says about life in the present day and about what is yet to come in the future.

You might wonder why proclaiming the Word is part of the image of God, but Adam's first failure was not in eating the fruit. He failed to proclaim God's Word to defend Eve from Satan. He failed in his duty as prophet, and thus, even though Eve eats the fruit first, the fault lies with Adam. This is why, with one exception, Scripture puts the blame for the fall of the world into sin squarely on him. Thus, anointing and Baptism seek to restore us to that duty and give us the knowledge of God needed to speak His will and Word into the sinful and unbelieving world.

Further in Depth

In Matthew 12:39–41, Jesus tells the Pharisees and scribes, "An evil and adulterous generation seeks for a sign, but no sign will be given to it except the sign of the prophet Jonah. For just as Jonah was three days and three nights in the belly of the great fish, so will the Son of Man be three days and three nights in the heart of the earth. The men of Nineveh will rise up at the judgment with this generation and condemn it, for they repented at the preaching of Jonah, and behold, something greater than Jonah is here." Jesus explains that Jonah's time in the belly of the fish relates to Christ's own death and resurrection.

Jonah's time in the fish certainly looks baptismal. After all, you've got someone being saved from death and a whole lot of water. Jesus' statement that it relates to His death and resurrection helps too, but taking a look at the story itself is the best way to see what Jonah's time in the fish is really all about.

If you take the time to read through the Book of Jonah—it's only four chapters, so it won't take you long—you'll probably remember a lot of the basic elements of the story. There's Jonah the prophet. There's God's command to Jonah to go preach to Nineveh. There's Jonah literally running away from God at every opportunity. God saves Jonah from drowning. Jonah goes to Nineveh finally and then has his pity party overlooking the city.

Jonah's time in the fish looks very baptismal. God saves Jonah from death. And yet salvation isn't really the point of the fish. Jonah *is* saved, true. But Jonah isn't saved so he can run off and do whatever he wants. Jonah is saved *so he can be a prophet.* God gave Jonah a job at the very beginning of the book. That hasn't changed. The job still needs to be done.

God saves Jonah so that he may carry out the task given to him: to proclaim His will to a pagan people. In this way, Jonah's salvation by the fish is very baptismal.

Looking at these different roles, we are led to the question of how we are restored to these roles. Certainly, this takes place in Baptism, but the question is *why*. Why does Baptism bring us back to these roles we were created to have?

To answer that, we remember what the roles of prophet, priest, and king all relate to: the image of God. We're again talking about creation, about the world as God originally made it. The first person who bore the image of God was Adam. Adam perfectly carried out all these roles, right up until he didn't. When he sinned, he abdicated these responsibilities, and creation became subject to disorder and death as a result.

In Romans 5, Paul tells us Adam's life was pointing ahead to Jesus. We often refer to Jesus as the Second Adam. Jesus relives Adam's life in many ways, but where Adam fell to temptation and brought sin into the world, Jesus would resist temptation and bring life. Jesus resists Satan at the beginning of His ministry. Jesus follows His Father's will perfectly. Again, we see those echoes of creation. Again, Jesus is busy resetting things to the way they were created to be. Jesus carries out the roles of prophet, priest, and king that Adam was meant to fill. Where Adam failed, Jesus will succeed.

Our Baptism restores us to that state of righteousness the world once had—a world only made possible through the life of Christ. He continues to carry out those roles in His perfect and sinless humanity. Our lives as prophets, priests, and kings or queens are a reflection of His. Our work in those roles is only possible because He makes it so by bringing us back to the righteousness we were meant to have.

Baptism restores our role in the world and then directs and empowers us to carry out that role.

Hymn Connection

"God of the Prophets, Bless the Prophets' Sons"

Text by Denis Wortman

This hymn is often used at ordinations and installations. It expresses some of the aspects of what God calls Christians to do. Though it doesn't explicitly refer to Baptism, it brings in the three different vocations that God anoints throughout Scripture together in one hymn. You may have sung this hymn before without really thinking about how this all comes to be. Now that we have looked at anointing and its connection to Baptism, you can see how God has made all this—not just for pastors, but for all Christians.

Questions for Review

16. As you think about your own vocation as a baptized prophet, priest, and king or queen, what does all that mean for how you interact with those outside the Church?

DISCUSSION NOTE: A prophet, priest, and king or queen all, by definition, have responsibilities in the world. Prophets are called to speak God's Word. God speaks of judgment and of grace. He directs His people to take His message to the world so that all may come to Him and find peace and salvation.

Kings and queens are tasked with helping the world to flourish by maintaining order and protecting it. That goes for not just the people inhabiting the world but also for the rest of it, for it was all created by God. Kings and queens care for the world, but even they need the guidance and support of their Creator. Priests hear the concerns of the world. So priests take the problems of the world to Him directly, asking Him to intervene in grace and mercy.

All this means there's quite a lot for baptized Christians to do. There is no sense in sitting around passively waiting for God to do things, for He has sent us to be His representatives and to love and care for His creation with our own two hands.

UNIT 5

Circumcision

Some of the major topics we've already touched on lead us to a new idea that comes into play when we talk about Baptism. To get a better feel for this new idea, let's take a look at another baptismal topic.

- Read Genesis 17:1–14.

1. What are the conditions of the covenant God establishes with Abraham?

DISCUSSION NOTE: At this point, Abraham and his wife, Sarah, have had no children together. God had told Abraham many years ago that he should move across the country to the land of Canaan, later known as Israel, to live there. Abraham had always had a large estate and been very successful, but he has no heir. In chapter 15, God promises Abraham he would have a son, but that was more than ten years ago at this point. Now God reiterates the promise He made. Abraham is older now, but that is still no problem for God. God now elaborates on the promise. Abraham will have a son and will go on to have many descendants, but there will be a visible sign among them that they are receiving the benefits of this promise. If they choose not to get circumcised, they have rejected the promise.

2. What does Abraham receive in this covenant?

DISCUSSION NOTE: The first item of significance here is the new name God gives him. Prior to this, his name was Abram, meaning "great father"—an unfortunate name for a man who was nearly one hundred years old and had no children. Now his name is Abraham, meaning "father of many." Abraham had been praying for a single child to carry on his lineage. God is giving him much more than he asked for: more descendants than can be counted.

3. **What is the significance of the time God requires for the covenant?**

DISCUSSION NOTE: God likes to repeat themes in Scripture. Often when you see a number repeated, there is something worth paying attention to. You might ask the participants if they can think of places where certain numbers get repeated. The number *7* gets used a lot, starting with creation. The number *12* comes up with the tribes of Israel and with the disciples. The number *8* does not show up very much in Scripture. So here, where it seems to be tied to something important, the number is either something with significance that is only known to God, or it is a new idea being expressed.

Despite the rather short passage, the connection between the covenant of circumcision and the Sacrament of Baptism is quite strong. Here God is claiming Abraham and his descendants as His people. Circumcision will be the mark by which the males will be known as the people of God. Their wives and daughters are even included in this covenant through the circumcision of the males. They are made different and distinct in this way. This is much the same idea as we saw back with anointing something or someone with the oil to make them holy and dedicated to God.

God is formalizing a relationship with Abraham and his descendants here. The people of the covenant will forever know they are God's people and that He is at work on their behalf. Should they reject the covenant, then they reject God. But unless that happens, they will always be His, no matter what else should befall them.

The time frame is also important here. A male child is to be circumcised when he is eight days old. While many theologians work out a defense of infant Baptism from the New Testament, the roots of this theology can be found right here. God claims a child only eight days old as His own. He doesn't simply offer it as an option or make suggestions here. He demands that it be done on the eighth day. God sees how necessary it is for His promise to come to each of us, even tiny babies. Circumcision is a command, just as Baptism is. However, it is a command that is tied to the promise of grace. God grants that promise of grace to all, even and especially to those who cannot even comprehend the magnitude of what they are receiving.

Modern medicine has found an interesting fact about circumcision in that the level of vitamin K that is necessary for blood clotting is not adequate to prevent a child from bleeding out during circumcision until he is at least eight days old.[15] Thus, circumcising a child before the eighth day could have serious consequences. So there is not only a spiritual component to circumcision but also a physical one.

In this case, one who is circumcised becomes a child of the same promise made to Abraham. This promise looks ahead to what God will later say as He declares the Israelites to be "a people holy to the Lord your God, as He promised" (Deuteronomy 26:19). He also tells them, "You shall be to Me a kingdom of priests and a holy nation" (Exodus 19:6). When God speaks to Abraham, He tells him he will be "the father of a multitude of nations" (Genesis 17:4). Now God carries the covenant with Abraham further and tells the Israelites exactly what it means to be His people. They are His. They are holy.

Looking back at Aaron's ordination, there's a similar time frame at work. His ordination takes place over seven days. For those seven days, he's confined to the tabernacle as he waits for the rite to be completed. It is

15 With modern medical advances and the vitamin K shot given to most newborns, baby boys can now be safely circumcised shortly after birth.

only on the eighth day that he actually begins his work as high priest over Israel.

Both circumcision and the ordination of the first high priest bring about a transformative change in the life of God's people. Each of them is taken from the people they were—people with no connection to God, no relationship with Him, and no ability to carry out the roles they were created to have—and each is made into someone new. Through circumcision, each Israelite becomes a child of the covenant and promise God made. Each becomes a recipient of everything God declared would be given to His people. Aaron becomes a priest again, with the privilege of coming into God's presence and of communicating the cares of creation to Him.

In Unit 3, I discussed how the eighth day on which it begins to rain in Noah's day might be an important connection later. Here we have found similar ideas coming together around the theme of Baptism. As with Aaron, there is a seven-day waiting period, then the big event actually commences. It might appear there's a difference in the activity since the eighth day is when Aaron begins working, and it is the eighth day when Noah is finally finished working, but this would be looking at it from the wrong direction. In both cases, the eighth day is when God begins working in earnest. Judgment for the world and salvation for Noah both enter on this day, while God also establishes a more intimate and interactive relationship with His people through Aaron.

Each of these looks to a restoration of creation, which would be suggested by the number 7, but then looks beyond it to something new. Let's explore this idea a bit more.

- Read Romans 6:1–11.

4. What does Paul mean by "newness of life" (v. 4)?

DISCUSSION NOTE: It is probably worth exploring what Paul is referring to here. Is it salvation, death, and resurrection? Or is it something else entirely? If the group gets stuck, you might suggest that if Paul were just talking about resurrection, he could have used that word. The fact that he doesn't might mean he's talking about something slightly different.

5. According to Paul, what role does Baptism play in our lives?

DISCUSSION NOTE: Consider what it means to be joined to Christ's death and resurrection. What does that entail? Does this somehow change who you are or how you live? If Jesus' life and death are yours now, what does that do for you? If your life is now Christ's, then when He dies, He is dying your death. He is living your life. When He rises from the grave, it is as if you had risen also. The only difference is that your physical resurrection hasn't actually happened yet.

Paul looks back on events such as circumcision to show us how sinners can be bound to God through the establishment of His covenantal promise. Had God not declared the significance of circumcision, the act would have meant nothing. But because of His promise, circumcision becomes the outward mark indicating that this Israelite belongs to God and is one of His people. Now Baptism carries on the same work in our lives by joining us to the life of Christ. We are baptized into the life of Christ. His death is our death through Baptism, so His resurrection will be ours as well.

Jesus Himself was circumcised in accordance with the command God gave to Abraham. He will go on to be baptized and, in so doing, bring together the Old Testament and the New Testament in His own life. Those who were circumcised were looking forward to the point when Jesus brings something new and greater into the world. He is the fulfillment of everything that has come before, so all believers in the Old Testament age are brought into the same promises we are because all are joined to the life of Christ.

However, Christ's resurrected life is not like His life before. Now, things like sin, death, pain, and sadness are all gone. He is a new person who has gone beyond death. Much of what we see in Christ's life is going through and reliving the life Adam was meant to live. This is why Paul describes Christ as being like Adam in 1 Corinthians 15 and Romans 5. But where Adam brought death, Jesus brings life. Jesus doesn't succumb to Satan's temptation, as Adam did. Jesus gives His life in service to His Father and to others, unlike Adam. In a sense, Jesus relives the world in the first days of creation, the world that was perfect until Adam and Eve gave in to sin.

On Good Friday, the sixth day of Holy Week, Jesus relives the creation of man and the fall into sin as He takes on the sins of the world and brings them to their natural conclusions: death. Jesus rests in the tomb on the seventh day of Holy Week, knowing His work is complete, just as His Father's work was completed on the sixth day and He rested on the seventh. When Jesus rises from the dead, He does so in a world that now has someone who lives beyond death. Jesus inaugurates the new creation with His own resurrection. The Early Church did not see the Sunday of Christ's resurrection as the first day of the week because the seven days of creation represent the old world that had fallen into sin. So Christ rises—not on the first day but on the eighth. This is the first day in a new creation that no longer follows the rules of the old one because here death is no longer a possibility.

Being baptized into Christ means following Him through death into new life. It means the new creation isn't simply something we wait for; it already exists in the life of Christ. Eternal life doesn't start when you die. You are already living it. God has promised you that life and has bound you to it through the covenant of Holy Baptism, which brings you into the life of His Son. Your resurrection is assured. It just hasn't happened yet. Baptism is the assurance of your resurrection. Luther says,

> Wherefore St. Paul, in Romans 6[:4], says, "We were buried with Christ by baptism into death." The sooner a person dies after baptism, the sooner is his baptism completed."[16]

16 Luther, *Luther's Works*, vol. 35, 31.

Baptism means death, but it is a death that brings you into something truly new. It brings you into a world where death no longer has any power. It is for this reason many baptismal fonts are octagonal. They show that you have entered into the new creation brought about by the new life of Christ. Each side represents a day of creation, with the eighth side reminding us of our connection to the new creation through Baptism. As we are joined to Christ's life in Baptism, we follow Him into that new world as well.

Further in Depth

One of the themes that crops up in Paul's letters is that of adoption. One such instance is found in Romans 8:14–17: "For all who are led by the Spirit of God are sons of God. For you did not receive the spirit of slavery to fall back into fear, but you have received the Spirit of adoption as sons, by whom we cry, 'Abba! Father!' The Spirit Himself bears witness with our spirit that we are children of God, and if children, then heirs—heirs of God and fellow heirs with Christ, provided we suffer with Him in order that we may also be glorified with Him."

The primary issue Paul is dealing with is explaining how those who are not descendants of Abraham can presume to call on God. In this particular passage in Romans, Paul makes an important point: if you have received the Spirit, then you are a child of God. It has nothing to do with whether you can claim Abraham as your ancestor and everything to do with whether the Spirit has come to you. Since the Spirit is a major player in the work of Baptism, anytime someone is talking about receiving this Spirit, it should make us think of Baptism.

Galatians 3:18 says, "For if the inheritance comes by the law, it no longer comes by promise; but God gave it to Abraham by a promise." In his commentary on that passage, Luther writes,

> This is undeniable, that before there was a Law, God by a promise granted Abraham the blessing or inheritance, that is, the forgiveness of sins, righteousness, salvation, and eternal life, which means that we are the sons and heirs of God and fellow heirs with Christ (Rom. 8:17). For Genesis clearly says (22:18): "In your Offspring shall all the nations be blessed." There the blessing is granted without regard for the Law or works. For before Moses was born or anyone had thought about the Law, God had already taken the initiative and granted the inheritance.[17]

Luther answers the question, "What is the relationship between God and his people?" His answer, expanding on Paul, is that the promise made to Abraham was always intended for everyone. The promise made to Abraham and expressed in the body through circumcision was a promise given to everyone. All nations will be bound together through Abraham's Offspring, Christ Jesus.

Baptism then answers the question, "How do we become joined to that promise?" The promise hasn't really changed. God still brings us into His family by means of His promise. In the Old Testament, that promise was bound to circumcision. In the New Testament, that promise is bound instead to Baptism. We receive the Spirit in Baptism, so everything that is associated with the Spirit becomes true for us as well. We are given the ability to call God "Father" because we are adopted through the Spirit in Baptism. We are children of God because He has claimed us as His own. Christ's own words in Matthew 28:19 that "all nations" should be baptized makes clear that this promise is not just for the Jews but for all people. None are excluded, regardless of their lineage.

I found this theology expressed strongly at the baptismal font in St. James Cathedral in Seattle, Washington. In a large marble square outside

17 Luther, *Luther's Works*, vol. 26 (St. Louis: Concordia Publishing House, 1963), 304.

the font are etched the words of 1 Peter 2:9: "But you are a chosen race, a royal priesthood, a holy nation, God's own people, that you may declare the wonderful deeds of God who called you out of darkness into marvelous light" (adapted from RSV). Though Peter echoes the words spoken by God to the Israelites, he is now explicitly applying them to the whole Church.

Rather than putting the emphasis on us and our public declaration of faith, as some church bodies will do, Peter is making it entirely about what God does for us. He has claimed us and made us His own. He has made the public declaration that we are His children. We now bear His mark on our foreheads and are His representatives, for we carry the family name Christian, which means "little Christ." Luther expounds on this a bit in his lectures on Titus:

> In Exodus (Ex. 19:5): "You shall be peculiar to Me, a peculiar people." We say, "My own," and Peter says (1 Peter 2:9) "a people for His possession." Vergil speaks of the *peculium*. That is, this is a people which is the property of Christ, in whose midst He dwells, which is devoted to Him, which He looks after as He would a flock, to which He has given life. Not only has He rescued it, but He purifies it every day if there is any filth left.[18]

The wording is a bit different, but the sense is the same. We are not just claimed as His children to be sent off on our own. God takes responsibility for us, cares for us, provides for us, and protects us. He puts His name on us and wants each of us individually and the world as a whole to know that we are His people.

Lutheran theologian Edmund Schlink has a brief thought as well:

> "All who are led by the Spirit of God are sons of God"

18 Luther, *Luther's Works*, vol. 29 (St. Louis: Concordia Publishing House, 1968), 67.

> (Rom. 8:14). Indeed, Christ is the eternal Son of God made man, and the Holy Spirit makes us His brothers who die and live with Him and in Him. He makes the believers adopted sons in Him, the incarnate Son. Not only are we "called" children of God, but we "are" so; not only shall we become God's children in the future, but we are that already (1 John 3:1).[19]

We don't need to wait until someday in the distant future, perhaps even waiting until we die, to be worthy of being children of God. Through Baptism, God makes us worthy now. Whatever we might think of ourselves before Baptism, from that point forward we can be confident of our status as members of God's household. Where before we were strangers, now we are His own adopted children.

Hymn Connection

"Baptized into Your Name Most Holy"

Text by Johann Jacob Rambach

This hymn expresses much of what Paul is saying in Romans 6. It uses Paul's own language and connects it to what takes place in Baptism on more levels. When thinking about weakness and lowliness in regard to the Sacraments, we are usually thinking in terms of sin and how we do not deserve what we are given. This is true, but it becomes an even more powerful message when applied to children, especially infants.

Genesis 17:1–14 explains how eight-day-old infants were circumcised and made a part of the covenant promise of God to His people. Not only are these infants sinners and unworthy of any of God's gifts, but they are physically powerless as well. A child that old has no power to earn Baptism or circumcision or even request it. This makes what they receive a gift in

19 Edmund Schlink, *The Doctrine of Baptism*, trans. Herbert J. A. Bouman (St. Louis: Concordia Publishing House, 1972), 62.

the purest sense of the word.

It also expresses some of what 1 Peter 2 declares as we receive His name and become His people. It is through this covenant promise that a Christian, whether child or adult, has God's name placed on him or her and can formally be considered a child of God. The hymn gives thanks for what God has done through Baptism. But it is also a prayer. It is a prayer that asks God to continue loving you as His own child and to help you learn and grow. It asks Him to help you stay true to the faith you have confessed through eternity.

Questions for Review

6. **Have you ever thought about your Baptism as a part of what makes you who you are?**

7. **How much does your Baptism affect your identity?**

God makes a definitive claim on you in your Baptism. You never have to worry or wonder where you belong from that point forward. You are God's child. You are a part of His family and are always welcome in His house. The whole rest of the world could abandon you, but God would still welcome you in with open arms. God stands by His promises and never fails to keep them. If He did fail to keep His promises, He wouldn't be a God worth worshiping.

This is what it means to be a child of God. He isn't a foster parent who is only signing up for a short time. He is adopting you and taking you as His own from this point forward. This relationship doesn't even stop at death. He signs up to be your Father forever and rejoices to share His home with you for eternity.

UNIT 6

Israelites in the Wilderness

Aside from the flood, the other Old Testament event most often reflected on as a basis for Baptism is the crossing of the Red Sea. Luther includes it in his Flood Prayer as well, saying,

> Almighty and eternal God, according to Your strict judgment You condemned the unbelieving world through the flood, yet according to Your great mercy You preserved believing Noah and his family, eight souls in all. You drowned hard-hearted Pharaoh and all his host in the Red Sea, yet led Your people Israel through the water on dry ground, foreshadowing this washing of Your Holy Baptism.[20]

In order to better understand the Red Sea, we should back up a bit and look at what led to the Israelites being at the Red Sea.

- Read Exodus 12:1–28.

1. What is the purpose of the blood on the doorposts?

DISCUSSION NOTE: There are a couple of ways to look at the significance of the blood. The first would be to see where it comes from. The lamb gives its life to provide the blood. The sacrifice of the lamb is a major component of the Passover, but that theology connects more closely to Communion than Baptism. Instead, think about what the blood on the doorposts says.

20 *LSB*, p. 268

What does it mean for it to be there?

2. **How does this use of blood relate to the rainbow after the flood?**

DISCUSSION NOTE: The placement of the blood is important here. In a sense, it even resembles the rainbow. It stands up over the people who gather together under it. If God is looking down at the people, He has to see them through the rainbow/blood. Look back at what the rainbow did for Noah, and the similarities start to become apparent.

3. **Why does God want them to continue celebrating the Passover in the future?**

DISCUSSION NOTE: It is worth noting the context of the Last Supper. Just prior to His institution of the Sacrament of Communion, Jesus was celebrating the Passover with His disciples. Even many centuries after the actual Passover event, Israelites were still observing the holiday. That suggests the message had an ongoing purpose. What is the message God is giving the Israelites that they are supposed to hold on to?

There's much in the Passover that relates to Communion, but for now, we're just interested in those things that tell us about Baptism. In this case, the blood on the doorposts functions in a very similar way to the rainbow after the flood. Here again, the blood is not meant for the people but for God. Judgment falls on the land of Egypt, but God sees the lamb's blood on the doorposts and remembers that judgment will pass by that house. The rainbow and the blood both remind God that any punitive judgment that needs to be given in this world is not going to fall on the people under the sign of the covenant.

The Passover event, like circumcision before it, continues to solidify the Israelites' place as God's people. They are the ones who were spared from God's judgment. God will repeatedly look back on the Passover-crossing event as the point that established them as His people. For example, in Exodus 20, God prefaces the Ten Commandments with the reason He has the authority to give them these commandments:

> I am the LORD your God, who brought you out of the land of Egypt, out of the house of slavery. (Exodus 20:2)

They are told to remember how this came to happen. Not that they repeat the same event over and over, for they are not in Egypt anymore, but that they remember how they escaped from Egypt to begin with. In this way, the Passover is already working like Baptism will later work for us in saving us from judgment and the death that goes with it, as well as giving us another way to be known as God's people. Let's take a look at what happens after the Commandments are given.

- Read Exodus 14:1–30.

4. What do Pharaoh and his armies represent here?

DISCUSSION NOTE: Pharaoh tells the Egyptian army to retrieve the Israelites and put them back into a position of servitude. We might more properly call it slavery, as God Himself says in Exodus 20:2. Slavery is already a bad way to live, but what's worse is that the country in general, and Pharaoh in particular, are openly hostile to the worship of the true God. That means the Israelites are slaves in a pagan land that cares nothing for them except as forced laborers until the day they die. Sin and death rule here.

5. Who receives this "baptism"?

DISCUSSION NOTE: Compare the crossing of the sea here to what happens in the days of Noah. Who lives and who perishes? Who goes through the water? In both cases, the details are very similar. Everyone involved is "baptized," but those who do not trust in God's promise end up perishing in the water.

Like the flood, everyone who enters the Red Sea is "baptized" here. The difference is that Israelites come through unscathed, while Pharaoh and his armies perish in the waters. For those who trust in God, the waters provide salvation. Everyone else finds only destruction here.

Pharaoh embodies unbelief and the power of death. He seeks to enslave the Israelites, crush them down, and destroy them. God shares with His people what Baptism is meant to do. By trusting in Him, we receive life instead of death and freedom from our sinful slavery to unbelief. What's also worth noting is that between the Passover and the crossing, God makes one very important point: "And when the Lord brings you into the land of the Canaanites, the Hittites, the Amorites, the Hivites, and the Jebusites, which He swore to your fathers to give you, a land flowing with milk and honey, you shall keep this service in this month" (Exodus 13:5). God doesn't just tell them that they are leaving but that they have a destination. There's a goal in mind from the very beginning: the Promised Land. From this point forward, God will lead them, and they will follow. In this sense, the Israelites have "died" to sin and unbelief and are living a new life as the people of God. We remember Paul commenting on this whole idea in Romans 6:6–7: "We know that our old self was crucified with Him in order that the body of sin might be brought to nothing, so that we would no longer be enslaved to sin. For one who has died has been set free from sin." While the crossing is significant on its own, it also leads us to consider the related event of the crossing of the Jordan.

- Read Joshua 3:1–17.

6. In what ways are the crossing of the Jordan and the crossing of the Red Sea similar?

DISCUSSION NOTE: Here is another place to compare and contrast. What makes the two events the same? What makes them different? Which of those details are important to the stories?

7. How does this event relate to the crossing of the Red Sea?

DISCUSSION NOTE: In both cases, the Israelites cross the water on dry ground. One key difference is that the Israelites are not being chased while they cross the Jordan. There are no enemies after them. Instead, as God reminds them, they are going into a land filled with people who will be hostile to them. Before, the unbelieving armies were trying to kill them. Now, they will be bringing the fight to the enemy.

Here, the Israelites cross a body of water on dry ground by the power and grace of God. In this case, they are not being chased by Pharaoh or anyone else. There is no threat of death. Nevertheless, this is not something they could have achieved on their own, and God has them go through this similar event to illustrate that the two events are related. All of the Laws of Moses were given to the Israelites while they were in the wilderness. The laws were given to help the Israelites learn what it means to live as the people of God and to give them a way to show, by word and deed, that they are not like any other group of people in the world. They are a holy people who have a special relationship with God. Their time in the wilderness is when they start to put this into action and begin living as God's people. It takes some time for them to learn how to do so, but they eventually get there.

All this time in the wilderness tells us something about our own lives as baptized children of God. We are made holy and are told through God's Word what it means to be His people. We learn to live as the people He has made us. We also have received our own promise and are looking forward to it. There is a new promised land, the kingdom of God, which comes into the world wherever Christ is. Thus, we look forward to His return. Baptism is what assures us we will be among the people who will be in that kingdom when it comes.

Israel's wandering in the wilderness for forty years recalls the forty days of rain during the flood of Noah's day. The wandering works similarly to the flood. It is an extended and thorough period of purification that washes people and creation alike to restore them and bring them back to what they were meant to be.

The forty-year journey was never the plan to begin with. God led the Israelites to the Promised Land rather directly from Mount Sinai. However, as they heard the reports from the spies they had sent into the Promised Land, they mistrusted God's abilities and gave in to fear. They ultimately refused the gift God was offering. All of this stemmed from sin. This sin necessitated the same kind of cleansing as the world did in Noah's day, so God leads them on a trek that purges that sinful mistrust from His people and binds them to Him. By keeping them in the wilderness for forty years, God is bodily removing the unbelief from the larger body of people. Obviously, the faithful who do pass into the Promised Land are still sinful, so this is not a complete purging of all sin. Still, it gives us an idea of how severely God deals with sin and how sin becomes a barrier between us and the promised land of the new creation we are looking for in our future.

This makes the two crossings and everything in between one long baptismal event. The people escape from death and unbelief in the Red Sea and are brought into the Promised Land through the Jordan. All the while, they learn to live as God's holy people and are distinct from the world. This tells us a great deal about what God has in store for us when we approach the baptismal font. He is saving us from a great many things, but He is also telling us what awaits us as we follow Him on the way to the promised land in God's new creation.

As I said in Unit 2, our Baptisms are only fulfilled in death. There, everything that God sees in us becomes reality. We look forward to our own promised land and await the day when our baptismal journey will be complete as we cross over to be in God's presence. In that sense, we are joined to the whole host of Israelites as they wander the Sinai Peninsula, following wherever God leads. During our journey, we will also learn to live as God's holy people, people who are distinct from the world around us. One day, as we follow Christ through our own grave and beyond, everything that God had begun in us here will be complete.

FURTHER IN DEPTH

I want to circle back around to the connection between the blood on the doorposts at Passover and the rainbow after the flood. In Galatians 3:23–29, Paul says,

> Now before faith came, we were held captive under the law, imprisoned until the coming faith would be revealed. So then, the law was our guardian until Christ came, in order that we might be justified by faith. But now that faith has come, we are no longer under a guardian, for in Christ Jesus you are all sons of God, through faith. For as many of you as were baptized into Christ have put on Christ. There is neither Jew nor Greek, there is neither slave nor free, there is no male and female, for you are all one in Christ Jesus. And if you are Christ's, then you are Abraham's offspring, heirs according to promise.

With that in mind, let's take the connection one step further. We recognize that the Law Paul is specifically referring to earlier in the chapter is the body of Law given to the Israelites through Moses. Paul is telling the Galatian Church about how God's promises work. The Israelites were not God's people because they kept the Law. The Law's main purpose, at least in Paul's current argument, is to point out how far we fall short of keeping it. Since we cannot keep the Law, it holds us captive.

In Galatians 3, Paul explains what makes someone a child of God. God promised Abraham he would have many descendants. One of those descendants would be the promised Savior, Jesus. Abraham wasn't told when all this would happen, just that it truly would happen. Abraham believed God, even though there was no evidence. This trust in God's promise is what makes you a recipient of that promise. The Law given through Moses to the Israelites much later did not make them children of God, for God had already established that through His promise.

We who trust in the promise of our Savior—not that He will come, but that He already has come and has given His life on our behalf—become heirs according to that promise. We become children of God just like Abraham and his descendants. Because we trust in God to provide a Savior, we are saved. In one sense, it is just as easy as that. We are given Christ's righteousness because we trust in Him to save us, and that's all there is to it. While we are saved through Christ, the wording Paul uses here suggests something more.

In Unit 4, we looked into the whole concept of the image of God. We talked about the roles we are given because we are made in the image of God and how the image of God isn't a physical resemblance but a spiritual one. Nevertheless, the wording is important. If I were perfectly righteous, then I would perfectly reflect all of God's love back to Him. Like a mirror, God would look at us and "see" the love He gave us coming back to Him. Since we are all sinners, we are all broken mirrors and do not reflect anything at all. We want to keep it all to ourselves.

This is where Paul's statement becomes important. In Baptism, we "put on Christ" (v. 27). While we are broken mirrors, incapable of reflecting anything, Christ has no such trouble. Christ is God, so by definition, He must be in the image of God. As one might put on a costume, we have put on Christ. So when the Father looks down at us, He doesn't see us at all. He sees only Jesus, and the love He has for us is perfectly reflected back to Him because Christ loves His Father—and all of us—perfectly. Thus, we are restored to the image of God, not because we have done anything special but because Christ is doing the job for us.

I bring all this up here because this passage also brings the rainbow and the blood together in the work of Christ. In my Baptism, I have put on Christ. That means all the promises made to me through Baptism are mine as well. God made a promise to Noah and all creation, and He made a sign of that promise in the rainbow. God made a promise to the Israelites, and He instructed them to make a sign of that promise in the blood of the lamb on the doorposts. When God looks at me and thinks about wiping creation out with a flood, He has to look at it through the rainbow, remembering the promise He made. When He threatened the nation of Egypt with the deaths of their firstborn males, He had to look at the Israelites through the blood of the lamb, remembering His promise. When He looks at me and thinks about bringing judgment against my sin, He has to look at me through Christ, remembering His promise.

Luther reflects on this a bit in his sermon on Romans 13 as he references this passage from Galatians 3:

> [Jesus] is our example and pattern, so that we follow Him and become like Him, clothed in the same virtues He is. About that St. Paul says that we are to put on Christ. Likewise, he writes: "Just as we have borne the image of the man of dust, let us also bear the image of the man of heaven" (1 Corinthians 15 [:49]); and "Put off your old man, which belongs to your former manner of life and is corrupt through deceitful desires, and be renewed in the spirit of your minds and put on the new man, created after the likeness of God in true righteousness and holiness" (Ephesians 4 [:22–24]).[21]

We exchange our dirty, sin-stained clothes for Christ's own robe of righteousness. Christ covers me completely.

The Father already inflicted the punishment for my sin on His Son. Now Christ is glorified and beyond death. Now He lives eternally. I am baptized, so I hide behind Christ. I don't want to come out of hiding, for that would mean I stand on my own, without protection. I would suffer the

21 Luther, "Epistle for the First Sunday in Advent," in *Luther's Works*, vol. 75 (St. Louis: Concordia Publishing House, 2013), 23.

same sort of fate as an Israelite who stepped outside during the final plague, no longer under the protection of the blood. Judgment would swiftly follow. "Putting on Christ" is one way to see how the promise becomes mine.

Hymn Connection

"Guide Me, O Thou Great Redeemer"

Text by William Williams

This hymn draws on the experience of the Israelites as they travel out of Egypt and make their way toward the land God had promised them. It was God who led them out of Egypt. God kept them safe on their journey. It was God who provided for them along the way. It was God who finally brought them to the Jordan and into the Promised Land.

The hymn expresses the sentiment of the Israelites, who put their trust in God to save them from beginning to end, acknowledging that God alone could make all this happen. It also makes the important point that should not be overlooked. In our role as priests, one of our responsibilities is to lift up praises to God, both our own and those of creation around us. We are people who have heard God's promises and trusted in Him. More than that, we have seen Him fulfill His promises. Praise is the proper and natural response we offer to God, thanking Him for all He has done for us.

Questions for Review

Consider what it means to "put on Christ." Think about what it means for Him to be living your life just as you live His. If Christ is living your life right alongside you, what does that say about God's willingness to help you through tough times? When you run into some difficulty this week, think about where Jesus is in all of it. What does His presence say about what's going on in your life?

From the time you are baptized, Christ's life and yours are bound together. He lives your life and dies your death perfectly. Unless you reject the grace given to you in Baptism, every moment of every day is one in which God sees His Son's righteousness covering you. The kind of love the Father has for His Son is given to you as well. If the Father gives life again to His Son, then He will do the same for you. In John 17:22–24, Jesus prays,

> The glory that You have given Me I have given to them, that they may be one even as We are one, I in them and You in Me, that they may become perfectly one, so that the world may know that You sent Me and loved them even as You loved Me. Father, I desire that they also, whom You have given Me, may be with Me where I am, to see My glory that You have given Me because You loved Me before the foundation of the world.

If the Father listens to the prayers of His Son, cares for Him, and glorifies Him, He will do the same for you. Prior to this, in John 16, Jesus tells His disciples, "Truly, truly, I say to you, whatever you ask of the Father in My name, He will give it to you. Until now you have asked nothing in My name. Ask, and you will receive, that your joy may be full" (vv. 23–24). The Father won't do anything to you or give you anything that would ultimately harm you. So He won't feed any sinful or selfish desires you might have. However, anything else you ask for, He promises to hear and bless.

UNIT 7

The Baptism of Jesus

The Baptism of Jesus is where all the elements we've examined so far start to come together. Each Gospel book mentions Jesus' Baptism, but none of them gives more than the essentials. Let's take a look.

- Read Matthew 3:13–17.

1. Who is involved in this scene?

DISCUSSION NOTE: It may be helpful to refer to Luke 1 to get a sense of who John is and what his purpose is here. It also is probably obvious, but it is important to put a name to the One who speaks from heaven.

2. Why is it important for each of those individuals to be present?

DISCUSSION NOTE: Jesus seems to think He needs to be baptized. Even if that is true, why do the Father and the Spirit need to be involved? What function do they serve here? John is meant to be the forerunner of Christ, the one who prepares His way. In baptizing Jesus, John is fulfilling his God-given purpose in announcing the beginning of Jesus' ministry.

3. Why does Jesus need to be baptized?

DISCUSSION NOTE: You may have ideas on why Jesus is baptized here, but from everything we've discussed so far, Baptism is to wash away sin. Jesus isn't a sinner and has no need to be made clean in this way. Some theologians will talk about how Jesus prepares the waters for our use, taking our sin on Himself, as it were. They are not wrong to think that way, but does this passage really talk that way, or is there more going on here?

4. How does this "fulfill all righteousness" (v. 15)?

DISCUSSION NOTE: If this is to "fulfill all righteousness," it might be worth discussing what *righteousness* means. We just discussed why Jesus needs to be baptized. Surely He does not need to be more righteous. So how does this further the cause of God's righteous work?

Taken all by itself, there just isn't a whole lot to go on here. Without looking at what has come before this point, we wouldn't have any idea why Jesus bothers to do any of this. John the Baptist is completely correct here. He is the sinner, not Jesus. A Baptism of repentance, such as John had been giving, or a new Baptism of grace and forgiveness, such as Jesus later commands, have no use for someone who has never sinned. But Jesus is not operating alone here.

This event is one of the few places we clearly see the Father, Son, and Holy Spirit all visible at the same time. Jesus, standing there in the water with the Father and the Holy Spirit around Him, should remind us of the very first time we see all three persons together: at creation. The Trinity does not appear here by happenstance. The triune God is actively demonstrating what Baptism is all about by recalling the very earliest point in history, when Father, Son, and Holy Spirit take an unformed ball of water and begin transforming it into the world we know. Baptism brings us back to creation, re-creating us into the sinless state and the image of God we were created to have.

This recalls Paul's statement in Romans 6:3–4: "Do you not know that all of us who have been baptized into Christ Jesus were baptized into His death? We were buried therefore with Him by baptism into death, in order that, just as Christ was raised from the dead by the glory of the Father, we too might walk in newness of life." We see here that being "baptized into

Christ Jesus" means a great deal more than just eternal life. Eternal life itself doesn't come about all by itself. Sin brings death. So sin must be dealt with so death ceases to exist. Thus, Baptism brings us back to creation, the time before sin. But it doesn't just bring us back to creation—it brings us to the new creation. It's not just a time before sin exists but a time when sin can *never* exist. Obviously, sin still exists today, but God no longer sees it and no longer treats us as sinners. He treats us as if the work begun in Baptism had already reached its fulfillment and we have been made completely clean.

Jesus is living the life Adam should have lived. He doesn't need to fulfill His own righteousness. He is fulfilling Adam's, and by extension, the righteousness of every sinner since. We are made righteous in Christ, and our Baptism has power because Christ prepared it for us. In the Large Catechism, Luther says,

> Therefore it is not simply a natural water, but a divine, heavenly, holy, and blessed water—praise it in any other terms you can—all by virtue of the Word, which is a heavenly, holy Word that no one can sufficiently extol, for it contains and conveys all of God. From the Word it derives its nature as a sacrament, as St. Augustine taught, "*Accedat verbum ad elementum et fit sacramentum.*" This means that when the Word is added to the element or the natural substance, it becomes a sacrament, that is, a holy, divine thing and sign.[22]

The triune God distills His creative and redemptive work into the water here. Just as God declares the anointing oil holy, to be used in making others holy, now Jesus claims the water as His, for making sinners holy and righteous. It should be noted that *Christ* and *Messiah* mean "Anointed One." All the references we saw earlier to anointing are applied now to Christ. The Church talks about Jesus as being a Prophet, Priest, and King, and here is

22 Large Catechism, Part 4, paragraphs 17 and 18.

where all of that happens. Through Him, we, too, become prophets, priests, and kings or queens through our own baptismal anointing.

The Spirit's presence here has a bit more for us to consider. Let's take a look at Jesus' later discussion of Baptism.

- Read John 3:1–8.

5. According to Jesus, what is the role of the Spirit in Baptism?

DISCUSSION NOTE: The Spirit has come up a bit in our study so far. Where have you seen the Spirit in the study before? Creation should come to mind. You might ask the participants where else they can think of the Spirit appearing in Scripture and whether any of those appearances relate to what Jesus is talking about.

6. What does Jesus mean when He says, "kingdom of God"?

DISCUSSION NOTE: If there is a kingdom, then there must be a king. Jesus is described as the King in the Gospel books, but no one seems to understand what sort of King Jesus is. Where is the kingdom of God, and how does someone come to be a part of it?

Here we find a Pharisee named Nicodemus doing what God's people were always meant to do. He goes to Jesus and seeks wisdom and understanding. Jesus' statements are confusing, but Nicodemus sticks with it in an effort to learn more, and he is not disappointed. Jesus spends some time talking about the Holy Spirit and what His role is in Baptism.

We saw the Spirit at Jesus' Baptism, but all we're told in the Gospel accounts is that the Spirit marked Jesus as the Messiah. Here, Jesus tells Nicodemus that the Spirit is integral to this notion of rebirth. In order to be "born again" (or "born from above," depending on how you translate the word), you need the Spirit.

This rebirth idea clearly confuses Nicodemus, but Jesus isn't saying anything new here. Looking at all the events we've examined, Jesus is just explaining again what Baptism does. If I am born with the sin of Adam, which means I do not have the image of God and can't fulfill any of the duties God created me to do, then I need to be born again, just without the sin. So Jesus tells Nicodemus that this is exactly what Baptism does.

The Spirit's role here might be a little puzzling too, but going back to Genesis 2:7 gives us the answer:

> Then the Lord God formed the man of dust from the ground and breathed into his nostrils the breath of life, and the man became a living creature.

The Hebrew word for *breath* is the same word they use for *wind* or *spirit*. So the Father puts His Spirit in Adam, and Adam comes to life. Thus, if I need to be reborn, it must be because I do not have the Spirit in me. Paul tells us this again in Romans 8:10–11:

> But if Christ is in you, although the body is dead because of sin, the Spirit is life because of righteousness. If the Spirit of Him who raised Jesus from the dead dwells in you, He who raised Christ Jesus from the dead will also give life to your mortal bodies through His Spirit who dwells in you.

In Baptism, we receive the Holy Spirit and are reborn. We are brought from death into life by the power of the Spirit.

Jesus makes Baptism a requirement for entering the kingdom of God. Throughout the Gospel books, Jesus constantly teaches about the kingdom of God. One of the biggest points He tries to get across is that His kingdom is not a physical kingdom with physical borders. His kingdom exists wherever the King is reigning. Since the King is Jesus Himself and Jesus is God, that means you need to be fit to be in the King's presence if you are to be in His kingdom. That means being cleansed of your sin. This is one of the major reasons Baptism comes before Communion since that is where you come into the physical presence of the King in the bread and the wine. In the next unit, we'll look at how Baptism comes to be a sacrament to begin with.

Further in Depth

In all this discussion of Jesus' Baptism and what He says about Baptism in John 3, we should take a moment and talk about the work of the Spirit a bit more as well. In both places, we see the Spirit at work in Baptism. Each person of the Trinity is involved in all aspects of salvation, but the Spirit often flies under the radar a bit. That's sort of His job anyway. He brings us to Christ, and all His work is geared toward bringing us in where the triune God is freely offering salvation.

That means the Spirit is very active in Baptism since it is one of the main gifts God gives to His people. We already talked a bit about the Spirit's role in bringing life. We confess in the Nicene Creed that the Spirit is "the Lord and giver of life," and His work in bringing what is inanimate and dead to life in creation and in re-creation is where that comes from.

The Spirit also brings us to faith. Faith trusts in God's promises, so faith is essential to being a disciple. Those promises are found in God's Word, and it is the Spirit who allows us to trust what we find there. Paul says this in 2 Timothy 3:16–17: "All Scripture is breathed out by God and profitable for teaching, for reproof, for correction, and for training in righteousness, that the man of God may be complete, equipped for every good work." I said before that in Hebrew *breath* and *spirit* are the same word. Though Paul writes in Greek, he is a Jewish scholar, and it is not strange at all to connect those two ideas here again.

God's Word carries along His Spirit so that wherever His Word is found, the Spirit comes along with it. That also means when God's Word is encountered either through verbal proclamation or through the written text, the Spirit is active and working in the one who hears or reads it. If the hearer is not yet a Christian, the Spirit is working to help him trust what God says to him in His Word. If the person is a Christian, then the Spirit is reminding her of what God has said and helping her to continue trusting in God and what He has promised.

Baptism builds on the foundation that has already been laid in faith. This makes what the Spirit does in bringing unbelievers to faith and what He does in Baptism related but distinct. We might say that once someone is baptized, the Spirit turns the volume up. God's Word is heard and understood more clearly because He has brought a greater level of restoration into the life of the baptized Christian.

The Spirit is active wherever the Word is proclaimed. The Spirit can engender faith and trust whenever someone hears the promises of God. We've seen how the Spirit does a great many things in and for God's people. How the Spirit works in one place is not necessarily how He works in another. The biblical themes for Baptism do connect with salvation, but they take what is given in faith and add even more richness and depth. It is as if what is given in faith is an outline, and now the Spirit begins filling in that outline with beauty and color. In Baptism, the Spirit gives our faith direction and purpose. Just as we saw in our discussion of anointing and the image of God, we are not simply saved. We are saved in order to do the work of God. The Spirit, who brought us to faith in Christ, now dwells within us to carry out the work we've been given to do.

When we looked at some of the extra elements of the flood narrative in Unit 3, one of the things that came up was a dove. The Spirit's appearance in the form of a dove at Jesus' Baptism is probably one you will recall a little better than the dove Noah sends from the ark. The dove in Noah's day is not something that will necessarily connect to anything in the future, for

God does not specifically tell us it will. But, like the numbers that show up in the passage we have already looked at, we should not be surprised to see the Spirit as a dove here.

In Noah's time, the dove comes at the end, as the floodwaters are receding. The judgment against sin has passed. Now creation has been restored to a state near what it was at the beginning. With that in mind, it comes as no surprise the form the Spirit takes here would be a dove. Jesus' Baptism indicates the time for fearing God's judgment against sin has also passed. Jesus' arrival and Baptism tells us He is here to live our lives as we were meant to. Since He is living our lives perfectly, we are safe from God's judgment.

Given that both events are baptismal in nature, the Spirit's form as a dove becomes a natural choice. Anyone seeing Jesus' Baptism who is familiar with the story of Noah should at least be thinking about where else the dove has shown up in Scripture. Since the word shows up nowhere else in Scripture except as poetic or figurative language, it becomes a pretty strong clue that the Spirit is directing people to the one other place a dove makes an appearance in Scripture. It should be obvious to those watching that what happened in Noah's day is somehow happening once again. Once, long ago, a dove indicated salvation was at hand, so a dove is once again telling people salvation has arrived.

We've talked about the number *40* already, but it shows up here again—not in Jesus' Baptism but immediately afterward. Jesus walks out in the wilderness to be alone for forty days. At the end of those forty days, Jesus is tempted by Satan. Though Satan offers Him many things, Jesus does not give in to the temptation.

Since Jesus is reliving our lives, getting right everything we get wrong all the way back to the beginning, we see a reenactment of the Garden of Eden. Satan arrives on the scene and begins twisting God's Word so as to introduce doubt and to offer things God has not offered. Where Adam and Eve gave in, Jesus does not. He makes it through the ordeal somewhat hungrier, but He is otherwise none the worse for wear. Satan tried his best and failed.

That Jesus does not give in here shows that Satan's lies cannot prevail against God. Jesus thwarts the tempter's power. Jesus undoes that first sin by reliving that event and getting it right. He defeats one of His enemies here and restores the original state of creation.

This is similar to how Jesus defeats death. The Early Church theologian Athanasius says, "Now if by the sign of the Cross, and by faith in Christ, death is trampled down, it must be evident before the tribunal of truth that it is none other than Christ Himself that has displayed trophies and triumphs over death, and made him lose all his strength."[23]

The Spirit aids all this work, and Scripture has alluded to this a couple of times. We've seen the dove active as Noah sends it out as the waters recede, but we actually see that Spirit-directed connection a bit earlier in that passage. Genesis 8:1 says, "And God made a wind blow over the earth, and the waters subsided." Where we see the word *wind*, the Hebrew reader again sees the same word as *breath* and *spirit*, or, more properly for us, *Spirit*.

Just like in the earliest moments of creation, where the Spirit hovered over the face of the unformed waters, here again, God sends His Spirit, and the work of creation begins anew as the waters subside. In the midst of the waters that brought death, God sends His life-giving Spirit to restore the world. The work that Christ will later do as He tramples down death is made known by the Spirit, who is a part of the process the whole time.

Lest we think this Old Testament, Spirit, and Baptism theme is just coincidence, God gives us another example. In Exodus 14, as the Israelites

23 Athanasius of Alexandria, "On the Incarnation of the Word," in *A Select Library of Nicene and Post-Nicene Fathers of the Christian Church*, Series 2, vol. 4 (Grand Rapids, MI: Eerdmans, 1957), 51.

are huddled at the edge of the Red Sea, watching Pharaoh's chariots rushing toward them, God sends yet another wind to part the waters. Yet again God breathes/*Spirits* into the waters and provides life and salvation in the midst of death.

Taken together with the dove imagery, God is weaving the flood and the crossing of the Red Sea together with Jesus' Baptism and showing us how many of the elements we have come to understand in Baptism have been there for a very long time. Baptism is not an afterthought of God or some sort of plan B. Baptism has been the goal all along, and the Spirit has been a part of it the entire time.

Hymn Connection

"To Jordan Came the Christ, Our Lord"

Text by Martin Luther

This hymn of Luther's may not be as well known as others, but it comes with some distinctive Luther trademarks. Luther often has a hard time getting everything he wants to say in just a couple of stanzas, so his hymns tend to be pretty lengthy. The seven stanzas of this hymn unpack the physical and spiritual aspects of Jesus' Baptism in the Jordan.

Luther first explains that Jesus came to the Jordan to be baptized by John. That might be an obvious comment, but the historical element is one of the aspects of Christianity that sets it apart from other religions. When we talk about Jesus being baptized and what that does for us, we aren't just talking metaphorically. Jesus truly did get baptized. This event stands in history as a true event to, as Jesus says, "fulfill all righteousness" (Matthew 3:15). Without the historical events, such as the flood or the crossing of the Red Sea, the promises God makes would have nothing to anchor to. We would have no proof that God does indeed fulfill His promises, and we would have no basis to trust Him for anything.

But those events did happen. Thus, all the themes we have explored, some of which Luther relays here as well, are all sure and certain. Baptism is a cleansing from transgression, an entry into new life, a joining of God's family, and more, all because God has established those themes and ideas and brought them together here with Jesus in the Jordan.

Questions for Review

7. **In what ways does the Spirit work through God's Word to guide you during the week?**

8. **How does the repentance and new obedience the Spirit works in you through Law and Gospel show He is active in your daily life?**

9. **What does His Word direct you to do?**

The Spirit is a part of Christian life every moment of every day. The Spirit is active in God's Word. So wherever God's Word is read and proclaimed, the Spirit is there. However, the Spirit is active in a more personal way when it comes to Baptism. As Jesus explains in John 3, those who are baptized are born again of water and the Spirit. The Spirit is within you, bringing you new life.

It is the Spirit who enables you to live once again in the image of God because it is the Spirit who brings you into Christ's life. The Spirit is always leading you to Christ. That means everything you do as a prophet, priest, or king or queen is directed by Him. That covers quite a lot of things. Some of those things are easily defined, like when you pray for someone or something, when you talk about God, when you care for someone else, or anything else like that. However, the Spirit is also simply helping you live more like Christ. Every temptation you avoid, every humble request for forgiveness, and every moment you find yourself trusting God is driven by the Spirit as well.

So aside from the tangible proof Baptism provides that the Spirit is with you, the Spirit continues to show Himself to you throughout your life. Any time you find yourself doing any of those things, the Spirit is there working in and through you. Paul says, "Therefore I want you to understand that no one speaking in the Spirit of God ever says, 'Jesus is accursed!' and no one can say 'Jesus is Lord' except in the Holy Spirit" (1 Corinthians 12:3). If you still trust in God's promises to save and give life, the Spirit is still with you. He works continually to keep you in the faith and to help you better live out your Christian life and calling every day.

UNIT 8

Discipleship

[Note to Leader: This unit will take what we've talked about and bring it into the Church's life today. Aside from the reading responses, the questions are designed for open-ended discussion. The answers will vary greatly depending on your church's circumstances and the experiences of the members. Encourage participants to draw on the themes and imagery that are a part of the study and think about how they might be used in your life today.]

It's great that God gives us so much information about what Baptism does, but until He actually tells us to do it, there's nothing tying His grace to the waters of Baptism. So let's take a look at what Jesus says about it.

- Read Matthew 28:16–20.

1. What are the two components of becoming a disciple?

2. What does Baptism consist of?

3. Why does discipleship only require these two things?

Teaching and Baptism are the dual requirements for discipleship. Jesus makes it surprisingly easy to hit the mark. Yet both requirements carry a great deal of weight. Through teaching and Baptism, Jesus calls each of us to do essentially what the Twelve did. They were taught by God Himself. They followed Him through His life and learned to put into practice the things He said and did. They learned to be like Him. But in order to carry out the things Jesus was saying and doing, they needed to be given the ability to do so.

Baptism has a great deal to do with justification—making us right in the eyes of God. It takes our faith and gives it a new focus and direction. Now we see Baptism also has a great deal to do with sanctification. It helps us to live the life God has always intended for us to live. With the Holy Spirit and the life of Christ within us, we are made to be like the people we were created to be.

Baptism itself is also quite simple. You have to draw a bit on the historical understanding of Baptism as a ritual washing, but Jesus changes it slightly by making it a washing specifically in the triune name of God. This, and only this, is the Sacrament of Baptism. Without a washing in the triune name of God, you have no Baptism. This is what God has promised will carry His grace and what will work the wonders He has prepared the world for.

With that in mind and as disciples of Christ ourselves, it's time to tackle some of the bigger questions.

4. Knowing what you know now, should the Church baptize infants?

Jesus doesn't specify whether you teach people about the faith and then baptize them (as usually happens with adults) or baptize them and then teach them about the faith they've been baptized into (as usually happens with infants). He only states that both need to happen for someone to be a disciple. So here Jesus doesn't differentiate between children and adults. All are commanded to be disciples through baptizing and teaching.

That alone is enough reason to baptize infants, but our study of Old Testament events gives us quite a bit more. Looking at how circumcision relates to Baptism, we see that God does not request but commands that eight-day-old boys be circumcised. As sinners, we do not naturally seek out God's gifts. We must be brought to a place where we can be put in contact with those gifts. Those boys are born bearing the curse of Adam, and through circumcision, that curse begins to be undone as they are formally made God's people.

The nature of that sin hasn't changed since the days of Abraham. We still bear the curse of Adam from the moment of our conception. We are not born as one of God's people. We must be made into one. God saw the need for this in Old Testament days, and that need is still there. Children need that promise as much as everyone else.

Since children are sinners, that also means everything related to the image of God and God's promises of salvation are there for them as well. Children still need the promise made through the rainbow and the blood of the Passover lamb that saves them from judgment and death. Children need the baptismal anointing so they can be prophets, priests, and kings or queens, just as God intended. Thus, children have just as much reason to be baptized as adults do. Children, too, are subject to death. They need to be joined to Christ's death and resurrection. That way, as they grow older and learn the significance of their Baptism, they will have that same concrete assurance of eternal life that God gives to all who come to the font.

5. How can we remember our Baptism after it has happened?

This is a question that doesn't have just one right answer. The Church has used many tools to help us remember how God is at work in our lives through our Baptism and to keep that work in mind even after we've been baptized. One tool is the sign of the cross. The sign of the cross is usually made on the ones who are being baptized to show that they are receiving the death and resurrection of Christ through their Baptism. That never ceases to be true. There are many places in the worship service that recall our Baptism, such as the Invocation, where we remember that it is the triune God who has invited us into His house, and it is He who put His name on us in Baptism.

The first half of the worship service, the Service of the Word, is built for disciples as well. This part of the service emphasizes God's Word and our response to it. This is the primary joy of disciples, and we are disciples through our Baptism. The worship service is designed to help us grow as disciples as we continue to learn from God.

The liturgical year is the Church's way of walking through the life of Christ. Just as the Twelve did in Jesus' day, we continue to walk through the life of Christ today. Listening to the words of our Lord and watching Him work is how we learn to speak and act as He did. All this draws on our role as disciples.

These are just a few places where our Baptism continues to flow through our lives in the world today, but there are many more. A thorough study of how God has prepared the world for Baptism will help us see how He continues to work in us and through us to make us His people. Baptism is truly a great and wonderful gift, such that God has spent a long time through the Old Testament developing the rich theology of the Sacrament for us to appreciate and use today.

6. Given what we've studied, are there reasons rebaptism might be acceptable?

The themes we've looked at state pretty conclusively that baptizing someone a second (or third, fourth, or even more) time simply doesn't make any sense. Circumcision, for instance, isn't something that is intended to be repeated (if that were even possible). Once you are a child of the promise, you remain a child of the promise, with all the attendant benefits and responsibilities. You may abdicate this role, but that doesn't change what God has offered to you.

The events of the flood or at the Red Sea are also not things to be repeated. In fact, in Deuteronomy 17, God forbids the people from returning to Egypt since that would mean a return to the sin and slavery He had saved them from. All these events worked to establish the people involved as recipients of His promises. God's promises never become invalid, and He never rescinds them. Thus, rebaptizing doesn't fit with any of the themes we've discussed. Rather, it runs very contrary to what those themes have communicated to us.

There are denominations that support or require this sort of practice. In some cases, this is because they only see Baptisms done in their churches as valid. The Lutheran Church does not hold this particular view. Jesus' command in Matthew 28:19 is that the Baptism be done "in the name of the Father and of the Son and of the Holy Spirit." Where water and the name of the triune God are present, there is a valid Baptism. Whenever a person has received a Baptism with water and the triune name, he has received a valid Baptism regardless of who did it. Since Catholics, Eastern Orthodox, and certain other denominations will conduct Baptisms this way, we have no problem with them and accept them just as we would a Baptism done in a Lutheran church.

Other denominations will see Baptism as a way of calling the Spirit to strengthen their faith and encourage them in their Christian living. While the Spirit is most certainly active in Baptism, this view implies that the

Spirit left, stopped working, or is waiting for the Christian to recommit before He continues.

The Nicene Creed affirms "one Baptism for the remission of sins." The Nicene Creed is one of the earliest and most universal confessions of faith in the Christian Church. It states that there is one kind of Baptism that offers this (a water Baptism done in the name of the triune God) and that this Baptism is only meant to be done once. The Creed was accepted by the Early Church because it clearly states what Scripture reveals. These ideas that Baptism can or should be done more than once only became widespread with reformers outside of Lutheran circles and were never a part of the Church prior to that.

7. **What sort of baptismal imagery can you find around your church? What sorts of themes do you see on display? Do these themes connect with other theological themes you see around your church?**

I mentioned earlier that many baptismal fonts are octagonal, alluding to the concept of the eighth day. Many fonts also have other images engraved, such as a shell or a dove. More elaborate ones may have Bible verses or a picture of Christ at His Baptism. The placement of the font and other images can also say something all on its own. Some churches will put their baptismal fonts right in front of the chancel so that the font is always in view. This suggests Baptism should be a constant reminder of what God has done and is doing in our lives. Other churches will put the font right inside the sanctuary or even just outside the entrance in the narthex. This reinforces the idea of Baptism as our entrance into God's kingdom and where we are adopted as His children.

Neither of these ideas is better than the other, but they do bring out different ways of looking at Baptism. There isn't a "right" place to put a baptismal font since the Bible doesn't speak to this. However, Baptism is meant to be a constant reminder of the grace God has given us.

You may also have pictures around your church referencing Baptism in one way or another. Some churches also commemorate Baptisms that have been done there on a banner or a bulletin board. It's not unusual to see a picture of Jesus' Baptism depicted in churches. Sometimes pictures of the Passover or the flood also make an appearance, but these are more rare. With the importance of the sacraments, we should always be challenging ourselves to find ways of making the sacraments and the theology that goes with them more prominent.

8. **Looking ahead, what could your church do to help members remember Baptism and think about what it does?**

9. **What are things you can do to help you remember the gifts given to you in Baptism when you're outside church?**

Further in Depth

Baptism is an important, even essential, part of Christian life. As such, it has a particular place and function in our lives. As in the case of issues like infant Baptism, if we misunderstand or misuse Baptism, it won't be able to carry out the full extent of what it tries to accomplish. The same is true of rebaptism. Practices like this end up muddying the waters, as it were, and confuse Christians about the purpose and scope of Baptism. This is why it is imperative that we take the time to study the sacraments in depth and learn how they provide the foundation for the whole life of God's Church.

The first part of the process for all Christians is the Holy Spirit creating faith in Christ our Savior through the Word and Sacraments. Paul says simply, "So faith comes from hearing, and hearing through the word of Christ" (Romans 10:17). Wherever God's Word is encountered, either through a church service, a quiet discussion between friends, or a Bible found in the drawer of a hotel nightstand, the Spirit promises to be active and at work, offering God's promises of forgiveness, life, and salvation. The Spirit works in the heart of the hearer to trust those promises. This trust is the essence of faith. The believer trusts that God can and will make good on what He promises.

Now that we've explored Baptism in depth, you can see that Baptism takes those promises and amplifies them. God gives concrete examples of forgiveness, of life, and of salvation. He shows us what that salvation looks like and, more important, what it means for us both now and in eternity. But like everything else God offers, it is a gift, a promise. Like someone offering me a Christmas present, I can accept what is given or I can choose to reject it, but I can't demand someone to give it to me. If I could, it would no longer be a gift.

The driving force behind the Sacraments is the same way God has always interacted with His people: through His Word. God's Word is what makes the Sacraments do what they do. God promises that when His name is used in connection with the water, all those baptismal gifts are a part of the package. In the Large Catechism, Luther says,

> It is often objected, "If Baptism is itself a work and you say

> that works are of no use for salvation, what becomes of faith?" To this you may answer: Yes, it is true that our works are of no use for salvation. Baptism, however, is not our work, but God's (for, as was said, you must distinguish Christ's Baptism quite clearly from a bath-keeper's baptism). God's works, however, are salutary and necessary for salvation, and they do not exclude but rather demand faith, for without faith they could not be grasped. Just by allowing the water to be poured over you, you do not receive Baptism in such a manner that it does you any good. But it becomes beneficial to you if you accept it as God's command and ordinance, so that, baptized in the name of God, you may receive in the water the promised salvation. This the hand cannot do, nor the body, but the heart must believe it.[24]

Seminarians will sometimes be challenged to explain why the church doesn't go out to ball games and amusement parks with water guns spraying everyone down and baptizing them. Forcing Baptism on someone is to try and force someone to accept a gift. What God offers is truly a gift. He doesn't force anyone to accept it, and neither should we. At the same time, Jesus' command in Matthew 28 also tells us teaching and Baptism go together. Someone who is baptized without any intention of being taught is disrespecting and misusing the gift God has offered. If they have no intention of becoming a disciple, then they are taking God's gift and then throwing it away.

If you continue your study of the sacraments, you'll see that Baptism (and all the theology that comes with it) is a lead-in to Communion. Communion builds on everything Baptism does. Without Baptism, Communion cannot operate in the manner intended. That means Christian life is a progression. God's Word is what powers all of this from beginning to end.

24 Large Catechism, Part 4, paragraphs 35 and 36.

Our lives are built around that trust we have in God's promises, both for our lives here in this world and into eternity.

All the baptismal themes we've explored involve salvation in one way or another. They all attest to the magnitude of what God has done for us. From the very beginning, salvation is always connected to faith. This doesn't change with the Sacraments. Salvation is still through faith alone.

The working of faith is one of those things we as Christians desperately try to make sense of, but it is not something within our power to determine or understand. That God holds the knowledge of how faith works is meant to be a comfort. He tells us very plainly how the Holy Spirit creates faith in us when we hear the proclamation of the Gospel—whether it is God's spoken Word or the Word working in and with the water of Baptism—and trust in the promise He makes to us there. Baptism doesn't save us because it is some kind of get-out-of-jail-free card. It saves us because Christ is the one using His Word in the water to build upon and strengthen our trust in God to care for us as His own.

John the Baptist's response to being near Jesus shows us that even an unborn child can trust in his Savior. A mother who goes to church before her child is born has already given her child the chance to hear the Gospel message and bring that child into the presence of his or her Savior. The opportunity has been given to that child to hear and respond just as John the Baptist did and to be saved.

Whether children die before or after Baptism, if they have been in the presence of their Savior and heard His promise to them, then we trust that the Spirit has been at work. We don't know what truly goes on in the hearts of anyone aside from ourselves. We don't truly know whether anyone else has faith or not. It isn't something God has given us to know or judge. What we do know with certainty is what Nehemiah and others throughout Scripture recalled: "But You are a God ready to forgive, gracious and merciful, slow to anger and abounding in steadfast love, and did not forsake them" (Nehemiah 9:17). God can and does have mercy on the weakest and lowliest, and He delights in doing so.

It's true that infants are unlikely to understand much of anything Scripture teaches, but knowledge is not the same as faith. Certainly, knowledge should be there, but that is part of the life of a disciple. Knowledge grows with time spent in God's Word as each of us is able to understand it. A baby simply hasn't had the time and doesn't have the ability to understand all of the theology of salvation. But a baby does know how to trust, which is the essence of faith.

Still, whether you came to faith as a child or as an adult, you probably don't remember the exact moment you came to faith. In this sinful world where doubts constantly assail us, you might start to question your faith. If you can't remember when you came to faith, then maybe that means you never really did.

This is why Baptism takes the form it does, as a single event in the life of each Christian. We don't know much about the faith life of Noah prior to the flood. As a sinful man, it's a certainty that doubts crept in regarding God's promise, whether He would send the flood and whether He would save Noah from it. The flood gave Noah something concrete he would always be able to look back at and remember. Whatever he was before the flood, at the very least from that point forward, he would know he was righteous in the eyes of God. He must be, for he wouldn't have survived otherwise.

Our Baptism does the same for us. Even if you can't remember the exact day and time you first trusted God's promises, Baptism makes that detail unimportant. God has claimed you in Baptism. He won't reject you or revoke His promise to you. That's why whenever Luther questioned his salvation, he would always recall that he had been baptized.

Baptism stands as a clear sign in your past that God has been and continues to be at work. Your Baptism is a reminder to you of what God has done. But it is also a reminder to God of what He has promised you.

As we saw in the first unit, Baptism is very much about forgiveness and salvation, but that doesn't mean it is identical to faith. God differentiates them for a reason. Baptism gives us more of everything God first offered through the hearing of His Word. Everything is bigger and more profound. Faith, Baptism, and Communion must each hold their own place for them to build up Christian life in the manner they are intended. Letting each do the job they were created for allows us to flourish and grow in the progression God has designed.

Hymn Connection

"O Christ, Who Called the Twelve"

Text by Herman G. Stuempfle, Jr.

Though this hymn refers more to the beginning of Jesus' ministry and His calling of the Twelve rather than the end, the purpose of the hymn is to describe the life of a disciple. The job of any disciple of Christ, whether one of the Twelve or any baptized Christian, is to follow in the footsteps of our Lord and Teacher. We go where He goes and do what He does. In so doing, we learn to be more like Him.

The hymn asks Jesus to do for us what He did for the Twelve. It asks Him to teach us as He taught them. It asks Him to help us learn what it means to share His love with those who need it and how to live a life of service to God and to our neighbor. It asks Him to strengthen our faith in times of doubt and strife so that we may stand fast. The Twelve did not figure out what they needed to do right away. They had their entire lives to learn what it meant to be disciples, for discipleship means a lifetime of learning. We ask Jesus to make us His disciples and to teach us our whole lives.

Questions for Review

10. What does the life of a disciple look like during the week?

11. How can you continue learning and growing in your faith outside of church?

The life of a disciple never stops, not even in death. Christ alone leads you from life to death to new life. He continues teaching us because we never stop needing to learn from Him. Church is the most important place because this is where Christ promises to be present with us. The service is the most important time because this is when He promises to be there. Our lives focus on those times we get to spend with Christ in person, but they don't end there. We are still disciples even outside of the church building. That means He continues to present us with ways to learn and grow spiritually.

We find opportunities to share the love of Christ with our neighbor just as Jesus' original twelve disciples did. They were learning to love others by watching their Lord and Teacher at work, and we carry on that same work today. This is also why we spend time in prayer and in the study of Scripture throughout the week. Christ is still speaking to us. Christ is always speaking to us in one way or another, even if it's just to remind us He's with us.